Conviction

K Owens

WESTBOW
PRESS®
A DIVISION OF THOMAS NELSON
& ZONDERVAN

THE HOLY BIBLE, NEW INTERNATIONAL VERSION®, NIV® Copyright © 1973, 1978, 1984, 2011 by Biblica, Inc.® Used by permission. All rights reserved worldwide.

Scriptures marked KJV are taken from the KING JAMES VERSION (KJV): KING JAMES VERSION, public domain.

WestBow Press books may be ordered through booksellers or by contacting:

WestBow Press
A Division of Thomas Nelson & Zondervan
1663 Liberty Drive
Bloomington, IN 47403
www.westbowpress.com
1 (866) 928-1240

ISBN: 978-1-9736-3607-6 (sc)
ISBN: 978-1-9736-3608-3 (e)

Library of Congress Control Number: 2018909333

Print information available on the last page.

WestBow Press rev. date: 08/21/2018

There are plenty of books out there about the Word of God. There are more than enough books available to make you feel good about your walk with God, and many preachers to soothe you with every sort of teaching known to man.

This is not one of those books.

I hope you read it and it helps change your life. I hope you put on your thick skin and open your mind to what God has been saying since the beginning of time.

I hope somewhere within these pages you're able to find what we need to complete our relationship with the Father and His Son, the beloved Christ:

CONVICTION

Preach the word; be prepared in season and out of season: correct, rebuke and encourage-with great patience and careful instruction.

For the time will come when men will not put up with sound doctrine;

Instead, to suit to their own evil desires, they will gather around them a great number of teachers to say what their itching ears want to hear...

2 Timothy 4:2-4

(NIV)

CHAPTER ONE

Judge Yourself

Of course, God loves you. But how do you actually rate as a child of God? Have you read the entire Bible for yourself? Or do you simply take the pastor of your church's word? What if he's some sort of nut who has a complete misinterpretation of scripture?

What if the people at your church are the kind who caused the fall of Jerusalem and begged the prophets not to preach anything bad to them and paid them to say there was peace and no coming wrath from the Lord? And what if your pastor is one willing to do so because he or she is more concerned with putting food on their table than preaching the truth of God?

I see a lot of preachers doing just that, and unfortunately, a lot of people prefer this type of message because no one wants to be inconvenienced in any way. It seems many want a pat on the back for doing just about nothing other than believing in God. Because of this, we can see the downfall of society, most purity in people slipping away, all fear of the Lord gone.

If you read My Soap, you'll see how I became a disciple of Christ and the Word of God. You'll learn about the pastor who, through his actions, showed me that one must read the Bible for themselves. That just because someone chooses the position of church leader, it is not an automatic that his or her actions and spirit are always reliable.

God's love is a free gift. But look at the other side of the coin. Does God really love you? Isn't it easy to tell yourself, and others, that God loves you no matter how big a piece of junk you are? But do you really believe it? And are you going to wait until Judgement Day and chance finding out that maybe God hates all sinners, especially the ones in the church, and that you've thrown your lot in with the wicked from day one?

Will you be one of those faux Christians who are going to burn down there with Satan because it was more convenient to give in to their fleshly desires and hold onto some false doctrine about an everlasting forgiveness from the Father God? Read the Bible, dear friends, because that is not what it says, especially not in the Old Testament.

So here are a few questions for you to answer to see where you rank on the going-to-heaven-or-burning-for-eternity scale:

1. Are you filled with true peace and joy or do you have to find ways to make yourself happy? Measure your depression level.
2. Is there a lot of strife in your life? Does it seem that bad things are constantly coming against you?
3. Do you think that you are a wonderful person? A God-fearing Christian?
4. Have you ever read the Word for yourself?
5. Do you commit big or little sins, seeming to always have to ask for God's forgiveness?
6. Do you periodically make a list of your faults so you can actually visualize them and work on righting them?
7. Are you comfortable in your sin, knowing God will always forgive you?
8. Do you often have to ask God for forgiveness for the same sin?
9. How much do you help others in need? Do you tithe?
10. Do you seek God's Word and live your life to do His will?

2 Corinthians 13:5

Examine yourselves, whether you are in the faith; test yourselves. Know you not your own selves, how that Jesus Christ is in you- unless you be reprobates. (KJV)

(Reprobates are people that are depraved, unprincipled, and wicked. People rejected by God and beyond any hope of salvation.)

So how did you do? Well, I hope. But just in case you found yourself lacking, let's go through the Bible and find out exactly what it says about the requirements for pleasing God. Because believe me, just saying, "Jesus is Lord" is not enough.

The scripture that changed my life and let me know that what I had heard preached was not the full message of God, was this:

Hebrews 6:4-6

It is impossible for those who have once been enlightened, who have tasted the heavenly gift, who have shared in the Holy Spirit, who have tasted the goodness of the word of God and the powers of the coming age, if they shall fall away, to be brought back to repentance, because to their loss they are crucifying the Son of God all over again and subjecting him to public disgrace. (NIV)

What does this scripture, in plain English, in black and white, tell us about forgiveness? It says that once someone receives the Holy Spirit and lives a life blessed by God's presence, they cannot come back to repentance because they knew better through the wisdom of God, and because Christ died so that they would have the strength to overcome.

I thank God for grace and forgiveness, but you cannot rely solely on that all your life-you have to grow in God's strength.

I notice that in this society we have taken our feel-good attitudes and turned them into a license to sin. And if you've read Jude, you will see that this was prophesied about two thousand or so years ago.

Jude 4

For certain men have crept in unnoticed, who long ago were marked out for this condemnation, ungodly men, who turn the grace of our God into lewdness and deny the only Lord God and our Lord Jesus Christ. (KJV)

Knowledge through grace and Jesus's death to know how to stay out of evil doings and knowledge of God's Word- which is His will- plus actually following His Word, will prevent us from falling into Satan's trap.

2 Peter 1:2-4

Grace and peace be multiplied to you in the knowledge of God and of Jesus our Lord, according as His divine power has given to us all things that pertain to life and godliness, through the knowledge of Him who called us to glory and virtue, by which have been given to us exceedingly great and precious promises, that by these you may be partakers of the divine nature, having escaped the corruption that is in the world through lust. (KJV)

Are you deserving of either type of grace? If God blesses you with His Holy Spirit, are you living a life that shows thanks for that gift? Or do you take this grace and abuse it?

Second, as in the scripture from Jude, one must remember it isn't always the mouth that denies Christ. Actions can also deny. And probably more so than mere words.

Titus 1:16

They profess that they know God, but in works they deny Him, being abominable, disobedient, and to every good work reprobate. (KJV)

Here Titus is speaking of those running the church. He says that they must be blameless since they are entrusted with the Word of God. He also says that there are many who are mere talkers and deceivers, and they must be silenced.

Jesus himself tells a story in Matthew 21:28-31:

"But what do you think? A certain man that had two sons, and he came to the first son and said, 'Son, go work today in my vineyard.'

"He answered and said, 'I will not,' but afterward he repented and went.

Then the father went to the second son and said likewise...

"'I go, sir,' he replied, but he did not.

"Which of the two did the will of his father?"

They said unto him, "The first." (KJV)

Sometimes words don't mean anything if the action contradicts what the mouth is saying. Like the decent people that do not yet profess the Name of Jesus, but by their actions glorify him.

Or the preacher who commits adultery and takes the monies tithed to the church. The millionaire who flies around in his own airplane, drives a Mercedes Benz, has three closets full of clothes, while half the world is starving, children are freezing for lack of clothing and shelter, people are dying and in need of aid yet they do nothing to help.

Helping others is where God's money and people's excess is supposed to go. We are told to take care of the poor, from Old Testament to New. Why do you need that million dollars? Why do you need another fancy building? How about housing for the poor and elderly instead? All that money could be used to help the homeless, feed the poor, provide Christian counseling; you hear of this being done by some churches, but it should be done on a much greater scale than it is. And the filthy rich rarely care for the people that are suffering in the world around them.

A lot of folks use excuses not to help people living on the street. "'If they weren't going to use it for drugs or alcohol I'd give them some money."

Remember, God didn't tell you to judge what that person is going to do with the money; you part with that piece of change and devote it to the Lord-because you are judged on your intentions as well as your actions. They will have to answer for what they choose to do with the money. You just be sure to praise God when you give it to them so they know where the money came from-not you, but from

God through you. A lot of good, reputable churches do, in fact, give generously to the poor. This is an important part of what a ministry should be doing.

But for those greedy people living the high life while God's children are starving, I have a parable that Jesus told just for them:

Luke 16:19-25

"There was a certain rich man who was clothed in purple and fine linen and fared sumptuously every day. And there was a certain beggar named Lazarus, which was laid at his gate and full of sores and desiring to be fed with the crumbs which fell from the rich man's table. Moreover, the dogs came and licked his sores.

"And it came to pass that the beggar died and was carried by the angels to Abraham. The rich man also died and was buried. And in hell, he lift up his eyes and saw Abraham afar off, and Lazarus with him. And he cried and said, 'Father Abraham, have mercy on me, and send Lazarus that he may dip the tip of his finger in water and cool my tongue, for I am tormented in this flame.'

"But Abraham said, 'Son, remember that in your lifetime you received thy good things, and likewise Lazarus evil things, but now he is comforted here and you are tormented.'" (KJV)

Now notice in this story it doesn't say that the rich man was an evil man. The only thing Jesus said was that the man was burning in torment because he was rich and didn't care at all for the poor man that was suffering right in front of his eyes. He kept all he had for himself, felt he couldn't spare a bit of anything, and so he was sent to Hades.

Giving to the poor is how you show thanks to God that you aren't in the same position.

And you're familiar with Jesus telling the rich man, "give all you have to the poor and follow me." The man wouldn't part with his beloved cash and so denied going with Jesus. And every time you hoard your money when you see someone lying in the street you do the very same thing.

So do the preachers of the Word that don't give, yet live in lavish surroundings and have million dollar churches while people lie homeless and starving. They may be in for a rude awakening when they stand for judgement. Especially if they also don't preach accountability for actions, and have people relying on God's forgiveness rather than living a life in goodness and love.

Of course, I'm all for tithing to your church. I believe in the principle of giving the first fruits of your labor. Just look at what happened to Cain. Because of his skimpy tithe and God's favor to Abel for Abel's wonderful tithe, Cain was moved to jealousy, killed his brother, and was banished from God's presence. That boy was gonna burn in Hades. And even his life on Earth was then tormented.

If you see another human in desperate need and you turn from him because you have convinced yourself that he will use the money for no good, and he dies from starvation, then you're a contributing factor. Your callousness and selfishness were the same motivations that led Cain to a greater sin.

Shouldn't the churches be helping these people in greater numbers? Find out where the thousands of dollars tithed to your church actually go. Is a new building more important than a man dying on the street? Which do you think is more important to God? And rather than another thousand-dollar suit or a second Mercedes, consider helping someone less fortunate then yourself. The Bible says it is easier for a camel to fit through the eye of a needle than for a rich man to get into Heaven. Living in great excess while so many are destitute is such a sin.

With mental illness crippling our society, consider donating somewhere for counseling to right the minds of people living in a prison of psychosis. Consider helping financially to fight against illegal drugs or human trafficking. It's the right thing to do. We have to care.

I love God with all my heart and do tithe to the church as much as I can, but a portion of my tithe goes to the homeless and those in need.

And I wonder what God thinks about people going to church to hear the Word of God and have a plate shoved in their faces to demand a tithe.

I think churches should do as Jehoida did when Joash was king- take a box, bore a hole in the lid, and place it by the altar (or the door) so people can give as their heart moves them. Do not beg in the Name of the Lord. People won't give any less money if they're allowed to tithe as they walk in. It shouldn't be a part of the service. The service is supposed to be about the truth of God, and the truth is, He isn't a beggar. That's the way He seems when the plate is passed around in His Name. People have definitely turned His house into a den of robbers. I don't like that God seems to be for sale- that is how the unchurched see Him with this practice.

In many cases tithing is another example of how actions and words fail to connect. God demanded that we take care of the poor and preachers should know this. They should preach this to their congregations so people can hear the whole message of God and go out and help mankind. But too often the usual reference to money is, "Give so we can build, buy, send, have."

And how does Christ end his story in Matthew 21? He sternly warns us that tax collectors, prostitutes, and the like will be accepted into heaven before any of the phony Christians will.

How do you think it looks to God and men when people that know better and have been blessed with God's power choose to stab Him in the back and do as they please knowing full well that it grieves the Father?

And in Matthew, Mark and Luke, Jesus speaks about grieving the Holy Spirit-important scriptures that are rarely preached.

Matthew 12:30-32

"He that is not with me is against me, and he that does not gather with me scatters abroad. Wherefore, I say to you, all sin and blasphemy shall be forgiven men, but the blasphemy against the Holy Ghost (Spirit) shall not be forgiven men. Anyone who speaks a word against the Son of Man, it shall be forgiven him; but whoever speaks against the Holy Ghost (Spirit), it shall not be forgiven him, either in this world or in the world to come. (KJV)

Also, Mark 3:29 and Luke 12:10

Here we see that perhaps there is not unconditional forgiveness for the children of God. Not a popular message because the human nature in folks wants to be whatever horrible creatures they feel like and still get to go to Heaven. But just think of the parables that Jesus told about the great banquet and the wedding banquet:

Matthew 22:2-14

"The kingdom of heaven is like a certain king who arranged a marriage for his son and sent out his servants to call those who were invited to the wedding; but they were not willing to come.

"Again, he sent out other servants, saying, "Tell those who are invited...all things are ready, come to the wedding." But they made light of it and went their ways- one to his farm, another to his business. And the rest seized his servants, treated them spitefully, and killed them. But when the king heard about it, he was furious. And he sent his armies, destroyed the murderers and burned up their city.

"Then he said to the servants, 'The wedding banquet is ready, but those I invited were not worthy. Therefore, go to the highways, and as many as you can find, invite to the wedding.' So those servants... gathered together all whom they found, both bad and good, and the wedding hall was filled with guests.

"But when the king came in to see the guests, he saw a man there who did not have on a wedding garment. 'Friend, how did you come in here without a wedding garment?' And the king had him bound hand and foot and cast into outer darkness where there was weeping and gnashing of teeth.

"For many are called, but few are chosen." (KJV)

This story tells of what has already happened with the Jews of old and the fall of Jerusalem, the acceptance of the Gentile into God's family; but it also warns about those who are not dressed for the occasion.

You are supposed to be wearing the blood of Jesus and the goodness of God. And if you're found to be clothed in the ways of the world or the Devil's garments-which are sin and self-servitude-then you are not going to be allowed to stay.

And another parable along those lines in Luke 14 tells where a man prepared a great banquet and the people he invited made a bunch of excuses. That man sent his servants to the streets and alleys to get the poor, crippled, blind, lame so the party would be full. Then angrily he said that not one of the people invited would ever get a taste of the banquet.

How honored are you to be invited into God's house? But do you rush to Him and show your appreciation, or are you too busy doing your worldly things to go? If you know what God has called you for, yet you continue in your old life because you are comfortable there, or you desire it so, then you're going to risk losing your seat at the great banquet and not even know what hit you.

Then Jesus said straight out in Matthew 7:21-23

"Not everyone who says to me, 'Lord, Lord,' will enter the kingdom of heaven, but only he who does the will of my Father who is in heaven. Many will say to me on that day, 'Lord, Lord, did we not prophesy in your name and drive out many demons and perform many miracles?' Then I will tell them plainly, 'I never knew you. Away from me, you evildoers!'" (NIV)

Your actions can deny Christ even if your mouth is saying, "Jesus is Lord." Except now that when your mouth says those precious words, your sin makes you a hypocrite. And I believe a hypocrite is far worse than an unbeliever. We are supposed to be God's chosen, God's examples, His representatives for the world to see. And what does scripture say about us now that we have the knowledge of God?

Hebrews 10:26-30

For if we sin willfully after we have received the knowledge of the truth, there remains no more sacrifice for sins, but a certain fearful look of judgement and fiery indignation, which will devour the adversaries of God. Anyone who has despised Moses' law died without mercy...Of how much more punishment will he be thought worthy who has trampled the Son of God under foot, counted the blood of the covenant by which he was sanctified unholy, and insulted the Spirit of grace? (KJV)

I almost had a heart attack when I read these scriptures in Hebrews. What little church I had ever had, had preached that message that you can sin, God is a god of love, you will always be forgiven. What a shock this was to know that all these years religious leaders had been helping to spread a message that kept people in a life of sin by simply telling them what they wanted to hear, what made them feel better.

In this they took away the fear of God, because the thought of not being right before Him is an undesirable one. It was not received well by the people, and the leaders wanted to keep their churches full.

However, reading this didn't make me feel sorry for myself. It gave me the conviction not to be one of those who re-crucified my darling Lord and Savior.

How much strength does knowing that that is exactly what I do every time I choose to sin give me? Enough to realize that I need to study God's Word, find out His desires and requirements, and start living a life worthy of the gift that I have received. Don't abuse grace.

It's a little uncomfortable for me to listen to preachers who try to smooth over sin in people's lives. "Oh, don't be too hard on yourselves, even though you're a piece of garbage, driving those nails in Jesus's hands, it's ok as long as you feel God loves you and you're happy with yourself."

Instead of worrying about their feelings, slam them with some truth and tough love; and if it motivates them to get their act together and stop sinning, their lives will turn around, and happiness and blessings will come.

We've got to preach strength and power and toughness rather than self-pity and self-indulgence.

I never understood that sinning made me an enemy of God. But doesn't that make sense? Go all the way back to Adam and Eve and see how sin separated them from God. And Cain, choosing to kill his brother out of jealousy, instead of just bucking up and doing the right thing to be in God's good graces.

How society is repeating the mistakes that led to the wrath of the living God going to the extreme of saying one can do any sort of evil and still go to Heaven.

Think of what caused the fall of Jerusalem. The people became so comfortable in their sin that they paid the prophets to tell them lies and prophesy nothing but peace.

Isaiah 30:9-11

These are a rebellious people, deceitful children unwilling to listen to the Lord's instruction. They say to the seers, "See no more visions!" and to the prophets, "Give us no more visions of what is right! Tell us pleasant things, prophesy illusions. Leave this way, get off this path, and stop confronting us with the Holy one of Israel!" (NIV)

As the story in Isaiah goes, the people had become a sinful nation (sound familiar?), a people laden with guilt. They had forsaken the Lord, spurned the Holy One, and turned their backs on Him. Every time we choose sin over the goodness of God we do the very same thing.

Isaiah 1:13,15-16

Bring no more futile sacrifices...your appointed feasts My soul hates. When you spread out your hands, I will hide My eyes from you; even though you make many prayers, I will not hear. Your hands are full of blood... Put away the evil of your doings from before My eyes! Cease to do evil, learn to do good!" (KJV)

It amazes me how a person can load themself down with sin after sin, and then wonder why God does not answer their prayers.

Isaiah 59:2-4

But your iniquities have separated you and your God; and your sins have hidden His face from you so that He will not hear. For your hands are defiled with blood, and your fingers with sin. Your lips have spoken lies, and your tongue mutters perverseness. None call for justice; nor do any plead for truth. They trust in vanity and speak lies; they conceive mischief and bring forth iniquity. (KJV)

Jeremiah 3:4-5

"Will you not cry to Me: 'My Father, You are the guide from my youth, will You reserve Your anger forever? Will You keep it to the end?' Behold, this is how you speak, but have done all the evil things you could." (KJV)

Although these are Old Testament readings, do not think that they don't stand today.

Now, I don't speak of the nonbeliever or the newly called. The unchurched are in a league of their own and all we can do is pray for them to find the grace of God. And baby Christians have a lot of learning and studying to do before righteousness can be expected of them. I equate them to the parable Jesus told in Luke:

Luke 13:6-9

"A certain man had a fig tree, planted in his vineyard, and he came and sought fruit on it and found none. Then he said to the dresser of his vineyard, 'Behold, for three years now I have come seeking fruit on this fig tree and find none. Cut it down! Why use up the ground?'

"And he answered, 'Lord, let it alone this year also, till I dig around it and fertilize it. And if it bears fruit next year, well! And if not, after that you shall cut it down.'" (KJV)

What do you think this parable means? What if it means that Jesus will tend our hearts for a time, but if we don't learn to produce goodness, we are of no use and do not belong in His family?

We are chosen out of the millions of other human beings on earth to be a joy and a blessing to God. We were not put here for Him to have to constantly forgive and cleanse us of the filth we so often choose to exist in.

Think of your own children. Did you give birth to them to have them be a constant source of pain and embarrassment to you? Of course not. What makes you think God doesn't have the same opinion of us?

There is a parable told by Jesus in Mark 12, and one in Luke 20, that tells us how this is in the eyes of God:

"A certain man planted a vineyard and leased it to some tenants and went into a far country. And in season he sent a servant to the tenants that he might receive of the fruit of the vineyard. But they caught him, beat him, and sent him away. And again, he sent another servant, they wounded him and treated him shamefully. He sent still another, and that one they killed; and many others, beating some, killing some.

"Having one beloved son, he sent him last, saying, 'They will reverence my son.'

"But when the tenants saw him, they said among themselves, 'This is the heir, let us kill him and the inheritance shall be ours.' And they took him and killed him and cast him out of the vineyard.

"Therefore, what will the lord of the vineyard do? He will come and destroy those tenants and give the vineyard to others." (KJV)

Do you continuously murder God's very own Son and our Savior? Your mouth may be calling yourself a Christian, but do your actions back it up?

At the end of these parables Jesus quotes the scripture referring to the stone the builders had rejected becoming the cornerstone, which is an important part of the foundation. And he is that stone. Your foundation should be built on Jesus and all his teachings, all his parables, not just the ones that we choose to pay attention to.

If you are living your life in sin and rebellion, you are rejecting Jesus and it may be a little tougher to get into heaven than you're believing it to be.

Isaiah 3:8

Jerusalem staggers, Judah is fallen; their words and deeds are against the Lord, defying His glorious presence. (NIV)

Don't just rely solely on forgiveness. Don't listen when some religious group tells you that you can do any horrible thing and get away with it.

What does the Bible say about forgiveness? What is forgiveness and who is entitled to it? The one in training and the sinner.

Ezekiel is one of my favorite books in the Bible, and it tells me exactly what I need to know about forgiveness:

Ezekiel 18:21-24

But if a wicked man turns from all his sins and keeps My statutes and do that which is lawful and right...all his transgressions he has committed will not be mentioned against him; in his righteousness he has done, he shall live...But when the righteous turn away from righteousness and commit iniquity and does the same abominations that the wicked man does, all of the righteousness he has done shall not be mentioned; because of his trespasses and sin, he will die. (KJV)

And again, in Ezekiel 33, we're told to turn from our evil ways. That a man's goodness will not save him if he is disobedient to God's commands. And also, that if an evil man turns from evil he will be forgiven.

Romans 3:25

God presented Jesus as a sacrifice of atonement, through faith in His blood. He did this to demonstrate His justice, because in His forbearance He had left the sins committed beforehand unpunished...(NIV)

Upon hearing these scriptures, don't consider yourself damned if you have been going to church and sinning all you want, because I doubt you've ever heard these verses. And even if you have, I doubt they were preached with any significance. I'm sure your righteousness was preached to you as a choice with little or no consequences for disobedience.

You've most likely always heard of God as a god of love, but believe me, He's no cream puff. He will not take lightly those who break His commandments.

How often, as a Christian, do you break the third commandment do not take the Lord's Name in vain? What do you think you do every time you sin? Your actions say that His Name, and the holiness and reverence that it inspires, mean absolutely nothing to you, or worse, that they only mean something to you when it is convenient to you.

Christianity is supposed to be a lifestyle. It is supposed to mean that you are a person of character, decency, strength, honesty. If you look at your thoughts and the actions you take in your everyday life, you will be able to tell quite plainly if you have the Spirit of God, or if you're one of those me, me, me, half-baked Christians. There is not supposed to be any middle ground with God and Jesus.

1 Corinthians 10:21

You cannot drink the cup of the Lord and the cup of devils; you cannot be partakers of the Lord's table and the table of devils. (KJV)

2 Corinthians 6:14

...For what fellowship has righteousness and unrighteousness? Or what communion has light with darkness? (KJV)

Yes, you are gifted with the knowledge of God and Jesus. Yes, you are blessed to receive the Holy Spirit. Yes, all the sins you committed before you received the Holy Spirit are forgiven. Yes, you have a bit of a free pass while you learn God's requirements. Yes, you need time to learn how to tap into God's power and yes, dear friends, you do live with the threat of damnation if you forsake and double-cross the Mighty God.

Luke 12:5

Fear Him who, after killing the body, has the power to throw you into hell! (NIV)

CHAPTER TWO

Law and Faith

Who do you think will be the most opposed to this message? In the old days, it was the chief priests, the teachers of the law and the elders, the men of the church, who opposed the message of holiness spoken by Jesus when he came and told them that not only were they worshipping in wrong manners, but that they were also leading their people astray.

Luke 20:19

And the chief priests and the scribes the same hour sought to lay hands on him...for they perceived that he had spoken the parable against them. (KJV)

And they also killed the other people of God who spoke it. They wanted to do as they had always done and not have it be wrong in the eyes of the Lord.

This was the main reason they killed Jesus, because he preached righteousness and purity to honor God. He told them that the laws they were following were nothing but the traditions of men, and that they had lost the truth of God.

The old Jewish leaders held themselves in such high regard that they refused to allow themselves to be touched by other people. That tradition died with Jesus's coming-all men were equal. They also wanted to eat only certain foods, be circumcised, follow all the special festivals and sabbaths-all of which God Himself had ordered an end to. It is these traditions that were the part of the law that were to be abolished, not the law itself.

1 Corinthians 7:19

Circumcision is nothing and uncircumcision is nothing. Only the keeping of the commandments of God. (KJV)

People are so excited about not having rules governing them that they have turned their backs on God's commandments and gone any old way they please. They figure that if they simply say, "Jesus is Lord," then they have allowance to do as they please and be forgiven. And who wouldn't want that: no pressure, no accountability, no repercussions. But it's just not so.

As a Christian, you have more responsibility to follow God's commands than you did before you received the Holy Spirit. You are no longer under the law because you are supposed to have in you a new spirit. You were supposed to have died to sin when you received it, and you are supposed to be led by righteousness, the righteousness of God and Jesus in you.

Romans 2:13

For not the hearers of the law are just before God, but the doers of the law will be justified. (KJV)

1 Corinthians 9:21

...though I am not free from God's law but am under Christ's law... (NIV)

Galatians 2:16

Knowing that a man is not justified by the works of the law, but by the faith of Jesus Christ... (KJV)

So, we understand that we are not under the law per say, but we live by faith. Faith is the root word of faithful.

If a parent warns a child not to run out in front of a speeding truck or they will get hurt, the child might believe the parent-they show faith that the parent speaks the truth. But they are not truly faithful until they heed the parents warning. If they are unfaithful, they may run out in front of the truck and get splattered.

Are you faithful to Jesus? What does he tell you to do to prove your faithfulness? Give your life to his teachings and to God.

Why would the man that would never rob the convenience store have to worry about the law that says he would go to jail for stealing? He would never rob the store in the first place, so he is not under that law. It is out of the goodness of his heart that he is free from it. That is the principle behind a Christian's freedom from law. For it says:

1 Timothy 1:8-10

We know that the law is good if a man uses it lawfully, knowing this: that the law is not made for a righteous man, but for the lawless and disobedient, for the ungodly and for sinners, for unholy and profane, for murderers of fathers and mothers, for manslayers, for whoremongers, for those that defile themselves with mankind, for men stealers, for liars and perjurers- and if there is any other thing that is contrary to the sound doctrine (of God). (KJV)

It is soundness of Spirit to believe that God expects holiness from us. It is not wise to risk your eternity on a misconception, an abuse of God's mercy.

If you are a Christian sinner or fit under any of the classifications mentioned in 1 Timothy 1:8, then you need to put yourself back under the law, because you are not living with the true Spirit of God. Do not in your over-confidence and exuberance forget about God's commandments.

Romans 3:31

Do we then nullify the law through faith? Certainly not! On the contrary, we sustain the law. (KJV)

The key is to make the law fill your soul, then you will no longer need rules.

Romans 3:21-24

But now the righteousness of God, apart from the law, is revealed, being witnessed by the law and the prophets. This righteousness from God, through faith in Jesus Christ to all who believe, for all have sinned and fall short of the glory of God, being justified freely by His grace through the redemption that is in Christ Jesus. (NKJV)

It's got to come from inside you. Your purity has to be a matter of your heart condition and not following the traditions of men. Even going to church is not going to get you into heaven, especially if:

A) You attend a feel-good church that has no truth or conviction:

1 Timothy 4:1-2, 7-8

The Spirit clearly says that in later times some will abandon the faith and follow deceiving spirits and things taught by demons. Such teachings come through hypocritical liars, whose consciences have been seared as with a hot iron.

Have nothing to do with godless myths and old wives tales; rather train yourself to be godly. For physical training is of some value, but godliness has value for all things, holding promise for both the present life and the life to come. (NIV)

Think of how much easier godliness will be when it is a state of mind and heart rather than forcing your body to obey some laws you heard. It must come from inside you naturally, not simply because you heard it from some man or read it in a book. You must know God's Word and let it permeate your whole existence. If you let your conscience receive the Holy Spirit's leadings, then you are living with a right heart. And that will be pleasing to God.

Deuteronomy 30:11-14

For this commandment which I am commanding you this day is not hidden from you, neither is it far off. It is not up in heaven... neither is it beyond the sea...but the word is very near you, in your mouth and in your heart so that you may do it. (KJV)

Or B) You hear the wonderful Word of God and leave what you heard right there in the sanctuary, not acting out the scriptures or serving God in your everyday life, thinking that that hour one day a week was enough to fulfill your commitment and guide you in the right direction.

In Isaiah 29, God warns that the people come near to Him with their words but not at all with their hearts. That their worship is nothing more than rule after rule taught by men and that it is all in vain.

Isaiah 30:1

"Woe to the obstinate children," declares the Lord, "to those who carry out plans that are not Mine, forming an alliance, but not by My Spirit, heaping sin upon sin." (NIV)

What is faith then? Is it simply believing that Jesus is Lord, or is there more to it? Take the scripture from Romans 10 about being saved:

If you confess it with your mouth, Jesus is the lord, and believe that God raised him from the dead, you'll be saved.

Suppose this verse was a mathematical equation, in its simplicity 2+2. But what if this verse was really algebra, which is a higher form of math, and the equation was actually 2+2 times Y? If you only concentrated on the uncomplicated 2+2 and ignored the harder portion, the times Y, you would end up with the wrong answer.

So to take those twenty-five or so words out of thousands and thousands of words and base your whole faith, your whole religion, and your whole eternity on them may not be a very wise thing to do.

Take it and break it down: If you confess with your mouth, Jesus is the Lord… The old saying goes, "Out of the overflow of your heart your mouth speaks." If you make what comes out of your mouth Jesus and his teachings, that will soon be what is in your mind. And if he is what is constantly on your mind, then goodness will soon become your natural actions. Submerse yourself in the Word.

"And believe in your heart that he was raised from the dead." If you believe that God has the power to raise a dead man from the grave, how can you believe that He doesn't have the power to keep you from sinning? That doesn't make sense. It's like saying you believe you can climb Mt. Everest, but you can't get out of bed in the morning. You can't believe the harder of the two and not what's easier for God.

Then, "You will be saved." A drowning man isn't saved until he is plucked from the water and placed on dry land. A believer isn't saved until he or she is plucked from that old life of sin and placed in righteousness.

In our faith in Jesus is the death of our sinful nature and therefore the need for the law.

Romans 6:1-15

We died to sin; how can we live in it any longer? For we know that our old self was crucified with Christ so that the body of sin might be done away with, that we no longer be slaves to sin- because anyone who has died has been freed from sin. If we died with Christ, we believe that we also live with him. The death he died, he died to sin once and for all; but the life that he lives, he lives to God. In the same way, count yourselves dead to sin but alive to God in Christ. Therefore, do not let sin reign in your mortal body so that you obey its evil desires. For sin shall not be your master, because you are not under law, but under grace. What then? Shall we sin because we are not under the law but under grace? By no means! (NIV)

We should no longer need to follow written laws because God's commandments are supposed to be written on our hearts-through faith in, and love of, Jesus.

God figured that people would desire to be Christ-like (anti-sin) and not use Christ's Name as a license to sin. But as in the old day, we've proven we need both Christ's Spirit as well as the law to get it right.

Like it says in Galatians, we must walk in love with joy and peace, treat others with kindness, be filled with goodness and faith, be gentle, and use self-control. Then there will be no need for the law. Those who belong to Christ have crucified their flesh and walk in the Spirit.

Galatians 4:9

But now, after you have known God- or rather are known by God- how are you turning again to those weak and beggarly elements? Do you desire again to be in bondage? (KJV)

Ephesians 6:6

Not with eyeservice, as men-pleasers, but as servants of Christ, doing the will of God from the heart. (KJV)

What does Jesus say about faith?

John 14:12

Verily, verily, I say to you, he who believes on me, the works that I do, he will do also. (KJV)

What did Jesus do as he roamed the earth? He spoke God's Word, he resisted all temptation, he taught love for all mankind, he kept the Lord's Sabbath Day holy, fed the multitudes, healed the sick and cast out demons.

Now we don't see much Hollywood-style demon possession anymore, but please realize if someone believes that they can sin all they want and still be in God's favor, they are in a fog put on them by an evil spirit. All sin is evil and harms the sinner. We must purge the evil from ourselves and others with the truth of God, the power of God in us that is able to resist sin.

Do not forget what was said to us:

James 1:14

...each one is tempted when he is drawn away by his own lusts and enticed. (KJV)

And

1 Corinthians 10:13

No temptation has overtaken you except such as is common to man; but God is faithful, He will not allow you to be tempted above what you are able, but with the temptation will also make the way of escape, that you may be able to bear it. (KJV)

Jesus will always be there. God made a promise and it will stand until the end of time. We're the ones who make the choice to live in God's love, or to follow the Devil's leading and give in to his temptations.

2 Timothy says that God did not give us a Spirit of fear, but one of power and love, and He gave us a sound mind. It's when people listen to the whispers of the Devil that they go off course. You can't

dwell on the bad thoughts that come into your mind. You must expel them with the joy of the Lord and the Word of God.

2 Corinthians 7:1

Therefore, having these promises, dear beloved, let us cleanse ourselves from all filthiness of the flesh and spirit, perfecting holiness in the fear of God. (KJV)

So, do not, in your laziness, believe any messages about in fact being a child of the Devil and calling, or thinking of yourself as, a child of God.

1 John 3:6-10

Whoever abides in Him does not sin. Whoever sins has neither seen Him nor known Him. Little children, let no one deceive you. He who practices righteousness is righteous, just as He is righteous. He who sins is of the devil, for the devil has been sinning from the beginning. For this purpose, the Son of God appeared that he might destroy the works of the devil. Whoever has been born of God does not sin, for God's seed remains in him; and he cannot sin, because he has been born of God. In this we know who the children of God are and who the children of the devil are: Anyone who does not do practice righteousness is not a child of God; nor is he who does not love his brother. (NKJV)

2 Corinthians 4:2

We have renounced secret and shameful ways; we do not use deception, nor do we distort the word of God. (NIV)

Colossians 2 says since you received Jesus, you must walk in him and watch that you are not taken captive through deceptive teachings that fit the world's ideals, not Christ's.

Many Christians do not want to hear anything about striving for or attaining any level of perfection. They just don't understand what perfection is in God's sight.

Psalms 19:13

Keep Your servant from willful sins, let them not have dominion over me. Then I shall be blameless, and I shall be innocent of great transgression. (NKJV)

Some Christians want to be similar to the unbeliever, giving in to their fleshly desires on a regular basis, but still believe that they get to go to Heaven. And a lot of preachers nurse them along, telling them not to feel bad about themselves and their shortcomings, which is giving strength to their weaknesses, rather than the power within them to overcome.

We need to stop feeling sorry for ourselves and do something to not engage in the sinful things that will ultimately grieve the Spirit and make us feel terrible and depressed.

And stop being overwhelmed with self-pity for having remorse, because you're supposed to; but use it for motivation to do the right thing.

Ezekiel 36:26, 31-32

A new heart I will give you and put a new spirit will I put within you; and I will take away the stony heart and give you a heart of flesh. Then you will remember your own evil ways and doings that were not good, and you will loathe yourselves in your own sight for your iniquities and abominations. Not for your sake do I do this, says the Sovereign Lord. Be ashamed and disgraced for your ways, O house of Israel. (KJV)

Everyone loves the idea that we, the church, are the body of Christ. And there are many scriptures attesting to this. We all know that Jesus is the head of this body and the believers make up the rest.

But say you're a pinkie and you get filled with an infection-which would be sin. If the diseased part of the body isn't healthy and doesn't heal quickly, then the owner of the body is going to be wise enough to amputate the sickness out of himself or the infection will spread like gangrene and contaminate the rest of his members.

This is why you are not supposed to be yoked with unbelievers, why you're supposed to expel the immoral brother (1 Corinthians 5), and most importantly, die to the sin filling each of you (1 Corinthians 15:30, Ephesians 2:1 and many more). So you don't pollute the holy body.

The pastor who cheats on his wife, lusting after all the women in his congregation; the priest who molests altar boys; the people in the congregation who sin all they want by gossiping slanderously, grumbling, and complaining all they can; the greedy preacher who misappropriates the church funds are all worse than the heathen because they are supposed to know better, supposed to have a spirit that wouldn't do these things. All of them are denying the truth through their actions, their end may not be what they believe it is going to be.

People think they are part of the Lord's body, but in too many cases, are worldly sinners doing all the evil they can. And if God cut off His chosen, what in the wisdom of the Word makes you think He won't chop your Gentile branch off too?

Romans 11:20-22

{The original branches} because of unbelief, were broken off, and you stand by faith. Do not be high-minded, but fear. For if God did not spare the natural branches, He may not spare you. Therefore, behold the severity on those that fell, but goodness on you, if you continue in His goodness. Otherwise, you also will be cut off. (KJV)

2 Peter 2:4-10

For God did not spare angels when they sinned, but cast them down to hell, putting them in chains of darkness to be reserved for judgement. And did not spare the old world, but protected Noah, a preacher of righteousness when He brought the flood on the world of the ungodly; and turning the cities of Sodom and Gomorrah to ashes and condemning them with an overthrow, making them an example of what is going to happen to those that live ungodly, but delivered Lot, a righteous man; God knows how to deliver the godly man from temptations and to reserve the unrighteous for the day of judgement to be punished. But mostly those that follow after the flesh and uncleanness and despise governing. (KJV)

Jesus himself said:

Luke 14:26-27, 34-35

"If anyone comes to me and does not hate...his own life, he cannot be my disciple; anyone who does not bear his cross and come after me cannot be my disciple,

"Salt is good, but if the salt has lost its flavor, how shall it be seasoned? It is neither fit for the land nor the dunghill; men cast it out. He who has ears to hear, let him hear." (KJV)

This warning from Jesus, includes not only what your worth becomes if you are a career sinner, but also an encouragement to hear the truth. And we have been warned about hearing the truth of things from the early prophets.

This is exactly what Jesus spoke of when he said:

Matthew 13:13-15

"Though seeing, they do not see; though hearing, they do not hear, or understand. In them is fulfilled the prophesy of Isaiah (6:9): 'You will be ever hearing but never understanding; you will be ever seeing but never perceiving.

"'For the people's heart has become calloused, they hardly hear with their ears and they have closed their eyes. otherwise they might see with their eyes, hear with their ears, understand with their hearts, and turn, and I would heal them.'" (NIV)

Sin is a sickness. It is part of the curse, and nothing impure will ever enter the kingdom of Heaven, nor will it be allowed to remain and infect the body of Christ.

Ephesians 5 says that no immoral or greedy person will enter the kingdom of God because a man like that is an idolater and we know that idolatry is one of the worst sins out there. We can't care more for how we feel than what would benefit or hurt others. That is idolatry.

That chapter also warns us not to let anyone deceive us with useless words because listening to stupid and misleading talk brings on the wrath of God.

Those who are polluted in the kingdom of Christ will be torn out and will never see the kingdom of God.

Hear these scriptures and repent for your sake and the sake of your children. There will be a judgment day and Jesus has been appointed as that judge. So if you are hearing today that you crucify Christ every time you sin against the Holy Spirit, how in the name of my precious God do you think you will not be weeded out?

We are told to use the Israelites' past as a warning about what will happen if we continue, as God's chosen, in our lives of sin. And what happened to His chosen by His avenging angels? He destroyed them along with their families, their homes, and even their temple.

1 Corinthians 10:5-13

But with many of them God was not pleased and their bodies were overthrown in the wilderness. Now these things are our examples to the intent that we should not lust after evil things as they did. And do not be idolaters...nor let us commit fornication, neither let us tempt Christ, do not murmur and complain. Now all of these things happened to them as examples and were written down for our admonition and warning. Therefore, let him who thinks he is standing (firm), take heed that he doesn't fall! No temptation has taken you but what is common to man. (KJV)

Ephesians 4:17-19

This I say to you, and testify in the Lord, that you do not walk as the Gentiles walk, in the vanity of their mind. Having their understanding darkened, being alienated from the life of God through the ignorance that is in them because of the blindness of their heart. Who being past feeling, they have given themselves over to lustful behavior, to work all uncleanness, with a greediness for more. (KJV)

Idolatry is to worship self or things-to sin against God, to make that buck, have that man or woman, spread that untrue gossip, get that load off your chest at someone else's expense and it's unacceptable for a seasoned Christian.

And preachers and priests feed this misconception with their offering of an abuse of grace, a reliance on repentance as merely asking for forgiveness. If you can simply say a few hail Marys, take communion, or ask forgiveness over and over and get away with all your sins, why not keep it up? You're pushing it and may end up with a mouthful in the end. Stop letting yourself be lied to and stop lying to yourself.

Matthew 23:23-28,33

Woe to you, you teachers of the law, you hypocrites! For you give a tenth of all spices but have neglected the more important matters of the law- justice, mercy, and faithfulness. You should have practiced the latter without neglecting the former. You blind guides! You strain out a gnat but swallow a camel. You clean the outside of the dish but inside are full of greed and self-indulgence. Blind Pharisee! First clean the inside of the cup and dish, and then the outside also will be clean. Woe to you, you hypocrites, you are like white-washed tombs, which are beautiful on the outside, but inside are full of dead men's bones and everything unclean. On the outside you appear to people as righteous, but on the inside are full of hypocrisy and wickedness. You snakes! You brood of vipers! How will you escape being condemned to hell? (NIV)

And along the same lines in Luke 11, Jesus also says to give what is inside you to the poor and it will make you clean. He is talking about caring for others, especially those less fortunate then we are. He also says that people neglect the love of God, which is the key to knowledge, again emphasizing that love is the basis of our walks. Jesus warns here that we will be held responsible for the blood of all the prophets from the beginning of time because by not acting in love, not only have we not entered into a proper walk, we have hindered those who were entering by not preaching love for others and an allowance of living a life of sin.

A Pharisee is one that is chosen by God, but who has turned his or her back on Him. And it was the Pharisees who helped crucify Jesus.

Look at your life; are you one? Are you a hypocrite and knowingly or unknowingly headed for damnation? Are you one of those who has convinced yourself that since by human works we cannot be saved, this would mean that none of your deeds matter? That is such a misconception.

You cannot go to Heaven by following mere traditions of men: circumcision, observing festivals, eating certain foods, being born an Israelite or Jew, washing your hands before you eat, not touching unclean people, going to church, saying, "Jesus is Lord." But believe you me, you will be judged on every deed, word, and thought, and if they are not acceptable in the eyes of God, you may be out.

Luke 21:34-36

"Be careful, or your hearts will be weighed down with dissipation, drunkenness and the anxieties of life, and that day will close on you like a trap. For it will come upon all those who live on the whole face of the earth. Be always on the watch, and pray that you will be able to escape all that is about to happen, and that you will be able to stand before the Son of Man." (NIV)

Do not convince yourself that what you do doesn't matter, that a few words are all that matter to God. God is concerned with peoples' hearts and you have to recognize that sin comes from the heart. If you know better in the first place, even if you feel sorry in the end, you have to try to use wisdom and a true love for God to avoid falling into sin.

Think power and strength. Try thinking about Jesus hanging up there on the cross with nails through his wrists and feet and see if that keeps you from the sin you are facing. Look at the length that Jesus went through to do the right thing. And we are also to go to such great lengths.

Hebrews 12:4

In your struggle against sin, you have not yet resisted to the point of shedding your blood. (NIV)

There are a lot of commandments that require time and knowledge to master. It seems you have some time to get in tune with your Holy Spirit, a time of learning and strengthening. But once you master something, if you turn back to that thing out of sheer self-indulgence, then you've shown what Jesus's death means to you.

And instead of feeling sorry for yourself after you commit sin, try shielding yourself beforehand with the wisdom, power, and love of the Holy Spirit.

Romans 2:5-6

Because of your stubbornness and unrepentant heart, you are storing up wrath against yourself for the day of God's wrath, when His righteous judgment will be revealed. God will give to each person according to what he has done. (NIV)

Galatians 6:7

Do not be deceived: God is not mocked. Whatever a man sows that is also what he will reap. (KJV)

2 Corinthians 10:5-6

Cast down imaginations and every high thing that sets itself up against the knowledge of God and bring captive every thought to be obedient to Christ. And be ready to punish all disobedience, when your obedience is fulfilled. (KJV)

What is pleasing to God? One who follows His commands. If you go through the big ten, you can rate yourself and see how you do.

ONE

I AM THE LORD YOUR GOD. YOU SHALL HAVE NO OTHER GODS BEFORE ME.

What is your god? Have you put sin and self-desire before the Holy One of Israel? Are you so anxious to be free that you have forgotten God and His commandments in the process? Do you not realize that following God is like being a slave? We were once slaves to sin, but with Jesus's death we became slaves to Christ and heirs to the kingdom of God, now needing to live our lives for God.

Everything you have and everything you are is His. Do not make yourself a god and obey your wishes over the Lord's. He is the only One and He alone will reign forever. Purposefully going against God's commandments and goodness is a form of idolatry and you shouldn't put yourself on any level near the Father. Just look at what happened to the one who tried to make himself equal to God.

TWO

YOU SHALL NOT MAKE AN IDOL IN THE FORM OF ANYTHING AND BOW DOWN AND WORSHIP IT

First, remember that the Lord said that arrogance is like the sin of idolatry (1 Samuel 15). What do you have over your worship of the Lord? Your life, your family, your possessions? Do you slave away for that house, that car, those clothes? Do you bow down to that boss and go against the Lord to do this man's will? Or some woman's will? Or Satan's will? Do you have little good luck charms? Are you up on the latest New Age techniques? Do you practice little rituals over true worship of God and ignore His desire that we be good and kind?

Is what you want more important than what God has decided should be? What do you look at physically and give in to that you know is against the Word?

This second commandment is where we learn the other side of God. For He Himself told Moses that He was a jealous God who would punish the children for the sin of their fathers to the third and fourth generation. So if you do not want to be decent for God or for your own sake, at least have the heart to think of your children.

THREE

YOU SHALL NOT MISUSE THE NAME
OF THE LORD YOUR GOD

If you are bold enough to call yourself by the holy Name of Christ and yet act like a child of the Devil, you misuse the Name. If you use the Lord's Name to get away with any sort of evil the devil parades before you, you are misusing the Name of God. If you call yourself a child of the living God and give in to every temptation that comes along, you have taken the Lord's Name in vain. That Name is one of power and strength, not weakness and ignorance. This commandment warns us that God will not hold anyone who misuses His Name guiltless. This is re-emphasized by Jesus in Matthew 12:30, Mark 3:29 and Luke 12:8; sinning against the Holy Spirit can be equated to misusing the Name.

2 Timothy 2:19

"...Everyone who confesses the Name of the Lord must turn away from wickedness." (NIV)

FOUR

REMEMBER THE SABBATH DAY BY KEEPING IT HOLY

This one is people's favorite to ignore. When we were told to no longer observe the festivals and sabbaths, people lumped the Lord's Holy Day in among them, but it was separate from the usual traditions of men and is still to be considered a sacred day.

The ten commandments are still in effect but are done out of love rather than as a requirement. And it's funny when people want to believe they can follow nine instead of all of them.

Isaiah gave us a guideline for God's Sabbath in Isaiah 58 that is relatively simple to follow. To keep from breaking the Sabbath; do not do as you please, you should call His day a delight and honorable, and do not go your own way or speak idle, useless, or vile words. Then God will be happy and you will find your joy in giving some effort to a simple request that we've been told to try to do.

We are supposed to follow Jesus by doing as he did and he followed the commandments and the Lord's Sabbath.

Matthew 28:1

In the end of the Sabbath, at dawn toward the first day of the week... (KJV)

God chose a day as His Holy Day. It was the seventh day, Saturday. I think we need to be careful about deciding which day we call His Holy Day. If He chose something, we should be cautious about deciding for Him which day that will be. God does not change His mind, don't make yourself a god and choose a day that is convenient for you or that has become society's norm over what God, Himself, has mandated.

FIVE

HONOR YOUR FATHER AND YOUR MOTHER

The Bible tells us that children should obey their parents because it is the first commandment with a promise. So even if you have a parent who lacks honor, it is in your best interest to be kind and considerate out of respect for God and the Word.

The dictionary defines honor as a showing of usual merited respect. So even if your parent is not honorable, you should always speak respectfully toward them, toward any elder. To any human being for that matter.

As a young child, you should try as best you can to obey what your parents tell you, as long as it is within the confines of the Word. As young adults, you should realize that God is your Father and since the coming of Jesus, we Gentiles became sons of the living God and should live lives honoring that acceptance.

You will never be free from obedience to a parent, but you will transfer your obedience from the people that birthed you to Father God, which should be your joy.

SIX

YOU SHALL NOT MURDER

In the beginning, God told Noah in Genesis 9 that He would demand an accounting from each man for his own lifeblood, and from every animal as well. He also said that He would demand an accounting for the life of our fellow man: whoever sheds the blood of a man, by men his blood will be shed, because we were made in the image of God.

Be careful about how you treat your body-any abuse self-inflicted. And watch what example you set forth for others.

We are to honor the life of all things and not kill for greed, or vengeance, or sport. Know that you will stand before the judgment seat and have to answer for every drop of blood that you have shed.

Try to make sure that your words don't cause horror or anguish in another person's life either. With your words you can kill the spirit in a person and we have a great accountability for our words. It is wise not to be hasty with the tongue and chance sinning against your brother.

SEVEN

YOU SHALL NOT COMMIT ADULTERY

You must control your lustful feelings. Keep yourself out of harm's way by staying out of situations that could lead to sin, which usually leads to heartache. And do not tempt others.

There is more to this verse than cheating on a spouse. We are told many times that Jesus is our husband and that at the end of it all he will come for his bride-the church.

2 Corinthians 11:2-3

...I promised you to one husband, to Christ, so that I might present you as a pure virgin to Him. But I am afraid that just as Eve was deceived by the serpent's cunning, your minds may somehow be led astray from your sincere and pure devotion to Christ. (NIV)

Remain true to the One who matters most. And you remain true by faithfulness in all matters.

EIGHT

YOU SHALL NOT STEAL

Of course you shouldn't take anything that doesn't belong to you, but you also should not rob people of the full message of God. And do not steal people's joy.

Give to the Lord what is His. Do not steal from Him what He has given you, including your time, your heart, your thoughts, your actions.

NINE

YOU SHALL NOT GIVE FALSE TESTIMONY AGAINST YOUR NEIGHBOR

Not only should you not lie about someone else, you shouldn't gossip about what they are doing either.

Remember what happened to Ham in Genesis 9. Noah became drunk and lay naked in his tent. Ham saw it and told his two brothers. But Shem and Japheth took clothing and laid it across their shoulders, then they walked in backward and covered Noah up.

They acted with respect and honored their father, and Ham was cursed because of the way he handled the situation.

Be careful about your opinions, be careful about judging others. Remember that with the measure you use to judge, it will be measured as judgement to you. And we're warned about judging the speck in our brother's eye when we have a beam in our own. How can we give testimony about another when we are no better?

TEN

YOU SHALL NOT COVET ANYTHING THAT BELONGS TO YOUR NEIGHBOR

If you see something that you would like to have, (say your neighbor buys a truck and you really like it), if you then buy one, you have committed no sin. But if you want it so much that you kill him for it, or treat him badly out of jealousy because of it, or do something against God to attain it, then it becomes coveting which is against God's command. But admiration and achievement at a normal level isn't a sin. Look at the proverbs that speak of work and reference to the ant and its labors for gain. It's okay to have things as long as they do not rule you.

John 13:34

"And a new commandment I give you: That you love one another." (KJV)

People so often want to believe that these words of Jesus's nullify God's commandments. But just because you introduce something new, that doesn't always mean that you no longer keep the old. Sometimes the new is just an extension of the old, especially when the new thing is nothing more than the old thing in a new package.

Jesus himself said that we do not discontinue following God's commands.

2 John:6

"And this is love: that we walk in obedience to His commands. As you have heard from the beginning, His command is that you walk in love." (NIV)

And when asked what the most important commandment was, Jesus said:

Mark 12:29-30

"The first of all commandments is, 'The Lord our God is one Lord. And you shall love the Lord your God with all your heart, and with all your soul, and with all your mind, and with all your strength.'" (KJV)

If you follow this command, you won't be doing anything against the Father's wishes or be giving in to the Devil's temptations. You need to find out how to really fall in love with God.

If you are madly in love with someone, truly in love with him or her, you naturally and quite easily make the object of your affection your first priority and never do anything to cause them grief. Find that for God. Don't just love Him when you're in church for an hour or when something is wrong. Love Him after you leave the church and before trouble gets you. Love Him enough to find out the truth and honor Him with your life.

It's hard to hear when people use the verse, "Love covers over a multitude of sin," and apply it to some sort of love from God that allows people to sin against Him over and over.

If you read the verses surrounding this particular line, you will find that the Bible is referring to our use of love to keep ourselves from sinning.

1 Peter 4:7-11

The end of all things is near. Therefore, be clear minded and self-controlled so that you can pray. Above all, love each other deeply, because love covers over a multitude of sins. Offer hospitality to one another without grumbling. Each one should use whatever gift he has received to serve others, faithfully administering God's grace in its various forms. If anyone speaks, he should do it as one speaking the very words of God. If anyone serves, he should do it with the strength God provides, so that in all things God may be praised through Jesus Christ. (NIV)

Nowhere in these verses does it refer to love by God. It is surrounded by instructions on how we are to act toward each other. If we love each other deeply, we won't sin against one another.

Jesus showed us his depth of love for God-he walked a pure walk and let himself be tortured and hung on a cross to do his Father's will.

Do you come anywhere near that? Or do you fold at the first breath of temptation or the first tinge of a bad mood?

The most important command of Jesus's covers the first four commandments. Then Jesus said to love your neighbor as yourself, which sums up commandments five through ten.

Remember in 1 John 2, John said that we know that a person has come to know God and Christ if they obey God's commandments. That the man who said he knew God but did not do what He commanded was a liar, and there was no truth in him. We must not hate others and we must not love the world.

1 John 1:5-6

...God is light; and in Him there is no darkness at all. If we say we have fellowship with Him and walk in darkness, we lie and do not live out the truth. (KJV)

1 John 5:2-3

This is how we know we are the children of God: by loving God and carrying out His commands. This is love for God: to obey His commands. (NIV)

Hebrews 4 says that we should have fear about getting to enter God's rest, we could fall short of the expectations for it. You have to mix the Word with your faith and obedience. And that some will enter that rest, but many who had received the gospel could not rest because of their disobedience. God says that if you hear His voice today, don't harden your hearts. Be open to all of what He says so that you can find peace, joy, and rest.

Faith is being faithful. Search your spirit and see if you are filled with true love for God and know and keep His requirements, or if you offer Him nothing but empty lip service.

Jesus, Himself, is quoted as saying:

Matthew 5:17-20

"Do you think that I have come to abolish the law or the prophets? I have not come to abolish them but to fulfill them. I tell you the truth, until heaven and earth disappear, not the smallest letter, nor the least stroke of a pen, will by any means disappear from the Law until everything is accomplished.

"Anyone who breaks one of the least of these commandments and teaches others to do the same will be called the least in the kingdom of heaven, but whoever practices and teaches these commands will be called great in the kingdom of heaven. For I tell you that unless your righteousness surpasses that of the Pharisees and the teachers of the Law, you will certainly not enter the kingdom of heaven." (NIV)

The law of the Lord is perfect,
    Converting the soul.
The testimony of the Lord is surer,
    Making the simple wise.
The statutes of the lord are right,
    Giving joy to the heart.
The commandments of the Lord are pure,
    Giving light to the eyes.
The fear of the Lord is clean,
    Enduring forever.
The judgments of the Lord are true and righteous.
They are more to be desired than much fine gold,
They are sweeter than honey and the honeycomb.
By them is your servant warned, and in keeping
them there is great reward.
                    Psalms 19:7-11

                        (KJV)

CHAPTER THREE

Repentance

What a blessing to have God's forgiveness. How do you show repentance? The Bible says in Acts 26 that repentance is proved by deeds.

People want to get so caught up in the fact that they are no longer under the law that they have thrown into their beliefs that their deeds no longer matter.

But know that although you are no longer accepted into the family of God by any of the works of your hands (circumcision, eating certain foods, etc.), and that you don't receive the Holy Spirit by anything you do, but acquire it by belief and faith in Jesus Christ, you will be judged on every deed you do, or do not do, throughout your Christian life.

As brothers of Christ, as children with the Holy Spirit, we are called to righteousness. And instead of being a lazy, weak, career sinner, why don't we stop feeling sorry for ourselves for the sin committed and work harder not to give in to the devil's temptations and start living a life worthy of the feel-good attitude we want to have?

Many folks want to feel no guilt and feel so great about themselves for doing nothing more than professing the name of the Lord. Well, until your actions and thoughts and soul and mind are righteous, you may not deserve to feel so great because you're misusing the Name, rejecting the truth, and crucifying Christ over and over again. Why should you feel good about that?

Have you ever thought that maybe you deserve the guilt that is heaped upon you? Maybe that depression filling your soul was brought on by your actions and is there because God has called you to be more than you are being.

Perhaps once you start changing your thoughts and actions into what is expected of a child of God, then, and only then, will that depression leave you.

Try doing it God's way before you let some preacher teach you how to find happiness in that life of sin. Don't listen when someone tells you to cheer up about failure in the eyes of God. Do it right and earn that happiness.

Why do you think you are shrouded in that sadness anyway? Have you read God's message spoken by Moses?

Leviticus 26:14-36

"'But if you will not listen to Me and carry out all these commands, and if you reject My decrees and abhor My laws and fail to carry out all My commands and so violate My covenant, then I will do this to you: I will bring upon you sudden terror, wasting diseases and fever that will destroy your sight and drain away your life. You will plant seed in vain, because your enemies will eat it. I will set My face against you so that you will be defeated by your enemies; those who hate you will rule over you, and you will flee even when no one is pursuing you.

"'If after this you will not listen to Me, I will punish you for your sins seven times over. I will break down your stubborn pride and make the sky above you like iron and the ground beneath you like bronze. Your strength will be spent in vain, because your soil will not yield any crops, nor will the trees of the land yield their fruit.

"'If you remain hostile toward Me and refuse to listen to Me, I will multiply your afflictions seven times over, as your sins deserve. I will send wild animals against you, and they will rob you of your children, destroy your cattle and make you so few in number that your roads will be deserted.

"'If in spite of these things you do not accept My correction but continue to be hostile toward Me, I, Myself, will be hostile toward you and will afflict you for your sins seven times over. And I will bring the sword upon you to avenge the breaking of the covenant. When you withdraw into your cities, I will send a plague among you, and you will be given into enemy hands. When I cut off your supply of bread, ten women will be able to bake it in one oven. You will eat but you will not be satisfied. You will eat the flesh of your sons and daughters. I will destroy your high places and pile your dead bodies on the lifeless forms of your idols, and I will abhor you. I will turn your cities into ruins and lay waste your sanctuaries, and I will take no delight in the pleasing aroma of your offerings. I will lay waste the land, scatter you among the nations and will draw out My sword and pursue you.

"'As for those that are left, I will make their hearts so fearful in the lands of their enemies that the sound of a windblown leaf will set them to flight. They will run as though fleeing from the sword, and they will fall, even though no one is pursuing them.'" (NIV)

Even though this was the warning God gave the Israelites long ago, remember that first of all, He did do everything He warned them He would do, and they came to ruin. And understand now that here in the United States we are living in Goshen, and look at the way society is deteriorating. Watch the news for an hour and see how these curses are beginning to overtake this coveted place on earth.

41

This scripture aptly applies to the way this country is becoming:

2 Chronicles 15:3, 5

For a long time, Israel was without the true God, without a priest and without the law...In those days it was not safe to travel about, for all the inhabitants of the land were in great turmoil. (NIV)

And this is what is happening again. We no longer have the true God; we are preached to about the one side of our Father, the side of love, but how can we forget the other side of Him? The side that destroyed Israel in the horrific way we read about in the Bible.

God is no pushover to be taken lightly. If you picture Him sitting on His throne sniffing daisies all day long you've only got half the picture. The truth is, He is also a consuming fire to be feared, and He will produce His wrath whenever it suits Him.

Then, we are, in most cases, without a priest to teach, because what good are half-truths and bold-faced lies? It's not often you hear about purity, hell, or wrath anymore.

And we are most definitely without the law because too often we're told that we can do any sort of evil and God will forgive us no matter what. But why risk that that may not be true? Wake up. Don't be one that waits until it is too late to find out.

Repent the way John and Jesus meant it-turn from that sin. Change your life, your way of thinking. Replace the accountability to God that has been smoothed over by slick priests and pastors and those who, whether with evil intent or unwittingly, keep you in your life of sin by telling you that you can be a child of God and a child of Satan all at the same time. It is just not true, and you're going to be sorry in the end, if you're not already.

Take a look at your life and see if you are living under God's curse or His blessings. How much do you sin against Him? How happy are you? Do you have true happiness or is it fleeting? Do you have to convince yourself that you're happy? Do you need outside stimulants to have joy?

It's time to judge yourself and get right with God. You must believe in yourself, that you can always do the right thing, that you have the strength. 1 Corinthians 9 says that we shouldn't run our race like people running with no end in sight. We shouldn't fight like people beating empty air with no purpose. We are to fight ourselves and make our flesh our slaves so that after we have preached to others, we will not be disqualified for the prize, getting to follow Jesus.

What good is carrying the Name of the Lord if you don't believe in all the things that having that glorious Name involves?

Purity and a right heart:

1 Corinthians 6:9-10

Know that the unrighteous will not inherit the kingdom of God. Do not be deceived: Neither fornicators, nor idolaters, nor adulterers, nor effeminate, nor abusers of themselves, nor thieves nor coveters, nor drunkards, nor abusive slanderers, nor extortionists, will inherit the kingdom of God. (KJV)

2 Corinthians 6:17

Come out from among them and be separate, says the Lord, and touch no unclean thing and I will receive you. (KJV)

1 Thessalonians 3:13

May He strengthen your hearts so that you will be blameless and holy in the presence of our God and Father when our Lord Jesus comes with all His holy ones. (NIV)

Hebrews 12:14

Follow peace with all men and holiness, without this no one will see the Lord. (KJV)

Matthew 5:48

Be, therefore, perfect, even as your Father, who is in heaven is perfect. (KJV)

Strength:

Isaiah 52:1

Awake...put on your strength, O Zion; put on your beautiful garments, O Jerusalem, the holy city. The uncircumcised and unclean will not come to you again. (KJV)

Acts 14:22

...We must go through many hardships to enter the kingdom of God. (NIV)

Romans 8:13

For if you live after the flesh you will die; but you, through the Spirit, put to death the deeds of the body, then you will live. (KJV)

2 Corinthians 4 reminds us that we are to be God's treasures, not failures. We should be like clay for God to form into the likeness of Jesus. That the power we possess is from God and not from our own strength. In life we are hard pressed with temptations from all directions, but never crushed by them. We are puzzled, but not to the point of discouragement. Persecuted, but not abandoned by the Lord who loves us. Because we carry in our soul the death of Jesus so that our life can glorify him.

Faith:

Mark 9:23

"All things are possible for him who believes." (KJV)

Hebrews 11:1

Now faith is being sure of what we hope for and certain of what we do not see. (NIV)

James 2:14-25 various

What good is it if a man claims to have faith but has no deeds? Can such faith save him? Faith by itself, if it is not accompanied by action, is dead...I will show you my faith by what I do. Faith and Abraham's actions were working together, and his faith was made complete by what he did...a person is justified by what he does and not by faith alone...As the body without the Spirit is dead, so faith without deeds is dead. (NIV)

If you have the power through faith to move a mountain (Mark 11:22-23), how can you not have the power to resist temptation?

Do you waste your prayers on financial gain, this thing or that thing, or do you start at the beginning and ask God for strength and wisdom?

I guarantee you that many of you need not concern yourselves with praying too much for everyone and everything under the sun but need to start healing yourselves and becoming true children of God. Pray for more of God's Spirit, and for holiness and righteousness.

Remember, God has mercy on whom He has mercy on, and He hardens whom He hardens (Romans 9). If you are a semi-believer, a Christian dabbling in all sorts of sin, then you need to find out why

God has not gifted you with complete faith. Something somewhere in your life is not right with Him and you had better find it and give it to Him to fix so you can be under His complete grace, and blessed with whole truths and overwhelming strength.

Don't be content with some pastor's sermon on Sunday and never seek God's Word on your own. What if that pastor is a hypocrite himself and is defiling those grounds, that sacrament, that Word? If he is not a holy man, then you could be going to a church that may dwell under a curse that his actions and black heart have brought on.

2 Peter 2:1-22

But there were also false prophets among the people, just as there will be false teachers among you. They will secretly introduce destructive heresies, even denying the Sovereign Lord who bought them...Many will follow their shameful ways and bring the way of truth into disrepute...Their condemnation has long been hanging over them, and their destruction has not been sleeping...They will be paid back with harm for the harm they have done. Their idea of pleasure is to carouse in broad daylight. They are blots and blemishes, reveling in their pleasures while they feast with you. With eyes full of adultery, they never stop sinning; they seduce the unstable, they are experts in greed- an accursed brood! They have left the straight ways and wandered off to follow the ways of Balaam (see Numbers 22), who loved the wages of wickedness...These men are springs without water and mists driven by a storm. Blackest darkness is reserved for them. For they mouth empty, boastful words and, by appealing to the lustful desires of sinful nature, they entice people who are just escaping from those who live in error. They promise them freedom, while they themselves are slaves to depravity- for a man is a slave to whatever has mastered him. If they have escaped the corruption of the world by knowing our Lord and Savior Jesus Christ and are again entangled in it and overcome, they are worse off at the end then they were at the beginning. It would have been better for them not to have known the way of righteousness, then to have known it and to turn their backs on the sacred command that was passed on to them. Of them the proverbs are true: "A dog returns to its vomit," and "A sow that is washed goes back to its wallowing in the mud." (NIV)

We must expect more of our religious leaders, as well as of ourselves. The church is supposed to be a holy establishment, a place of purity and refuge. How good can it be if it is defiled by the one set to lead it? Jesus is our example of the appropriate leader of a church.

Ephesians 5:25-27

...Christ loved the church and gave himself for it that he might sanctify and cleanse it with the washing of water by the word, to present it to himself as a glorious church, not having spot or wrinkle; but that it should be holy and without blemish. (KJV)

Ephesians 4:20-24

You, however, did not come to know Christ that way (**through sin**). Surely you heard of him and were taught, with regard to your former way of life, to put off your old self, which is being corrupted by its deceitful desires; to be made new in the attitudes of your minds; and to put on the new self, created to be like God in true righteousness and holiness. (NIV)

In 2 Corinthians 6 we are told not to put any kind of stumbling block in anyone's path or it will discredit the ministry. Instead, since we are servants of God, we should walk in the power of God, with endurance in purity. And we're supposed to speak truthfully, so, make sure you know what the whole truth of God is before you think to advise others.

Have you ever heard or read this Scripture?

Matthew 13:41

The Son of Man will send out his angels, and they will weed out of his kingdom everything that causes sin and all who do evil. (NIV)

Here we learn that Jesus will be in charge of the renovation of the chosen. How happy do you think he is going to be with you if you've been crucifying him over and over again?

If you're one of those who allow yourself indulgences and just ask forgiveness whenever it suits you, what if he comes at the exact time you're committing that abomination against him and the Father? Do you think he's going to turn his back and say, "Oh sorry friend, let me just hold off until you've finished, then I'll do my judging?" Fat chance brother.

For Jesus himself said:

Matthew 24:36-44

"But of that day or hour no man knows, not the angels of heaven, but my Father only. As in the days of Noah, so will the coming of the Son of Man be. For as in the days before the flood, they were eating and drinking, marrying and given in marriage, until the day that Noah entered the ark; and they knew nothing until the flood came and took them away.

"Watch, therefore, because you do not know what hour your Lord will come. But know this: If the man of the house had known at what time the thief would come, he would have watched and would not have allowed his house to be broken in to. You also be ready, for the Son of Man will come at an hour when you do not think he is coming." (KJV)

1 Thessalonians 5:4-5

But you, brothers, are not in darkness so that this day should overtake you like a thief. You are all children of light and of the day. We are not of the night, nor the darkness. Therefore, then let us not sleep like the others, but let us watch and be sober. (KJV)

Don't waste your time trying to decipher when the end of all things is coming. We must simply live decent lives and not worry about when Jesus will appear. So many eagerly await the end, but Jesus said you are to dread that time, probably because so many that think they are going to Heaven have been fooling themselves and are going to be condemned.

Everyone wants to think they will be taken up immediately, many want to consider themselves saints, but if they look at their lives then many will find that they are nowhere near as saintly as they believe themselves to be and may have to go through some of the horror of John's revelation because they haven't done 100% right by God.

The story I hear preached the most is the one of the prodigal son in Luke 15, about how he left his own land with his inheritance, squandered it, and came back with his tail between his legs. Upon his return, his father threw him a great banquet and welcomed him back with open arms. But a very interesting point is never recognized in the summation of this parable and that is; how many times did the boy leave? Once. He only left one time and was smart enough to know the sorrow and pain of being away from his father's house.

Many take that story and tell it as if it pertains to the continuous coming and going of Christians in and out of the presence of God, but the boy left once.

And how many times did Jonah have to get swallowed by the whale before he did God's will? He was also smart enough to only need one slap on the hand. How many times is God going to have to crack the whip on your back before you give a little effort to truly serving Him?

Hebrews 9:24-26

For Christ did not enter a man-made sanctuary that was only a copy of the true one; he entered heaven itself, now to appear for us in God's presence. Nor did he enter heaven to offer himself again and again, the way the high priest enters the Most Holy Place year after year with blood that is not his own. Then Christ would have to suffer many times since the creation of the world. But now he has appeared once for all at the end of the ages to do away with sin by the sacrifice of himself. (NIV)

Remember, repentance is turning from your sin, not just asking God's forgiveness and keeping your old ways. There are repercussions for that kind of Christianity.

In Luke 13, Jesus tells the people to repent or perish.

He also said:

Luke 13:24-29

"Make every effort to enter through the narrow door, because many will try to enter and will not be able to. Once the owner of the house gets up and closes the door, you will stand outside knocking and pleading, 'Sir, open the door for us.' But he will answer, 'I don't know you or where you came from.'

"Then you will say, 'We ate and drank with you, and you taught in our streets.'

"But he will reply, 'I don't know you or where you came from. Away from me all you evildoers.'

"There will be weeping and gnashing of teeth there, when you see Abraham, Isaac, and Jacob and all the prophets in the kingdom of God, but you yourselves are thrown out. People will come from the east and west and north and south and will take their places at the feast in the kingdom of God." (NIV)

These scriptures say that many will try to enter. The only ones that will be trying will be those who know about it, those in the church, and it says that many will not be getting in.

Jesus also said in John 4:23 that a time is coming when the true worshippers will worship the Father in spirit and truth, that they were the kind of worshippers the Father seeks.

What is the truth about the sin in your life? It is the spirit of the Devil and has no place in a child of God.

Jesus said:

John 8:34-35

"I tell you the truth, everyone who sins is a slave to sin. Now a slave has no permanent place in the family, but a son belongs to it forever." (NIV)

Then he goes on to say:

John 8:43-47

"Why is my language not clear to you? Because you are not able to hear what I say. You belong to your father, the devil, and you want to carry out your father's desire. He was a murderer from the beginning, not holding to the truth, for there is no truth in him. When he lies, he speaks his native language, for he is a liar and the father of lies. Yet because I tell you the truth, you do not believe me! Can any of you prove me guilty of sin? He who belongs to God hears what God says. The reason you do not hear what God says is that you do not belong to God." (NIV)

And over and over again Jesus asked us to walk as he did, serve God as he did, to persevere and overcome for the glory of God and in the strength of His awesome power.

In many chapters in John, Jesus conveys his thoughts about serving God. Principles like people who have done good will rise to live, but those who have done evil will rise and be condemned. That his sheep listen to his voice. He knows them, and they follow him. Also, that we know the way to the place where he is going.

The way to Heaven is not through sin. From the beginning of the Word, we have learned that sin leads to death. Do you believe that that has changed because you say, "Jesus is Lord"? Because that is not what Jesus himself said. He reinforced the old sayings.

There is so much more to being a child of God than a few catch phrases. There is accountability, responsibility for the gift of being one of God's chosen. There is a walk you must walk. There is an entire message of love.

What do you think Christ died for? To give you an out when you chose to sin? No. He died to fulfill the prophets. He died as the last blood atonement. He died so we could receive the Holy Spirit. He died so that the hearts of God's chosen would be revealed. He died to put an end to sin. He died to show the extent to which we must go to do the Father's will and resist temptation.

Do you think Jesus was tempted to run for the hills when faced with torture and that hideous death? He was flesh and blood. Remember in Gethsemane how distressed and grieved he was? But so as not to sin he prayed to God and said, if there was any way the cup could be taken from him, that'd be great; but that not his will, only God's will be done.

How often do you stand up against your trials and temptations and feelings? Or instead do you give in to them right away because perseverance doesn't feel good?

How do you think Jesus felt as they beat him, spit in his face, hated him, pounded nails through the tender parts of his wrists and feet? Then hung him on a cross to bleed to death? Why don't you picture what he went through while that sin is parading itself before you?

The next time you want to feel sorry for yourself, imagine having to go through what Jesus did for God. All we are asked to do is be decent and kind and loving. Not much of a sacrifice is it?

My brothers and sisters in Christ, if you do not stop sinning, you are not my brothers and sisters in Christ.

Every time you come to that fork in the road-and the second you wake up in the morning you're faced with it-always choose the godly path. A short time later, you'll be faced with another challenge. Again, choose the righteous course and pretty soon, you will show God that you are truly making an effort. And you'll be rewarded.

You'll receive more of the Holy Spirit, more strength to overcome and before long, following the correct path will become second nature. Then you won't feel guilty because you are finally living your life for God.

So, which is wiser; choosing sin and having to ask forgiveness then trying not to feel guilty all the time or toughening up and trying it God's way and having a real reason to feel good about yourself and your walk with God?

If you think that God does not hate, and will not hold a grudge, and that He can't get angry beyond extending forgiveness, there is one everlasting example that shows that this is, in fact, not true: Satan.

Satan will never enter into God's kingdom because he refuses to walk in the ways God set before His creations. And Satan was the morning star to God, but now he is burning in Hades for all of eternity.

So don't convince yourself that a few words will save you. You must join them with action that attests to the fact that God's words rule your life.

Even at my most righteous, if my walk is humanly perfect, God is so unfathomably holy that I am still filthy to Him. So, if saintliness is filthy to God, what do you think a born-again sinner is in His eyes? Bad fruit. And what do we learn happens to those that bear bad fruit?

Luke 3:7-9

John the Baptist said to the multitude coming to be baptized by him, "You generation of vipers! Who has warned you to flee from the wrath to come? Bring forth fruit worthy of repentance...The ax is laid at the root of the trees, every tree that does not bring forth good fruit is cut down and cast into the fire." (KJV)

And Jesus warned:

Matthew 18:7-9

"Woe to the world because of the things that cause people to sin! Such things must come, but woe to the man through whom they come! If your hand or your foot causes you to sin, cut it off and throw it away. It is better for you to go through life maimed or crippled than to have two hands or feet and be thrown into the eternal fire. And if your eye causes you to sin, gouge it out and throw it away. It is better for you to enter life with one eye than to have two eyes and be thrown into the fire of hell." (NIV)

This is the extent to which we are to go to prevent ourselves from sinning.

Do you think that Jesus said these things because he liked to hear himself talk or do you think there is a threat of damnation still in effect like he warns?

He also said:

Matthew 8:11-12

"I say to you, that many will come from the east and the west and will sit down with Abraham, Isaac, and Jacob in the kingdom of heaven. But the children of the kingdom will be cast out, into outer darkness, where there will be weeping and gnashing of teeth." (KJV)

Many, many people who think they are wonderful children of God might be in for a rude awakening on the day of Judgement. Over and over Jesus and the prophets in the New Testament call on us to be pure, decent, and void of sin.

In Acts 10, Peter tells us that God does not show any favoritism and He accepts men from every nation. But it is those who fear Him and do what is right whom He accepts. There is a path we must walk that is described over and over in the Bible by Jesus and all the prophets from Old Testament to New.

Isaiah 35:8

And a highway will be there; it will be called the Way of Holiness. The unclean will not journey on it; it will be for those who walk in the Way... (NIV)

Tough hearing isn't it? The only one who doesn't want to hear that drugs are bad for you is the drug addict just as a believer is comfortable in his or her life of sin until someone teaches them and shows them that it is against the Way. So be careful how you receive this message. If your defenses shot up immediately and you denied the truth of purity, judge yourself and see if you do, in fact, live a life of sin.

I wrote a little saying a long time ago that didn't have too much significance until I read the entire Bible for myself and learned the whole message of God.

"I would hate to be the fool who waits until it is too late to find out."

We need to step back, put self-pity aside, and look at our lives. See if you are living under a curse. How are things going for you? Then you need to analyze your life and determine why.

What might you be doing that is against God to bring it on? Are you a straight-out sinner or do your sins creep along behind you? The harsh or unnecessary judgment of others, laziness, rebellion, no love for mankind. Start being honest with yourself about yourself.

But if you truly find nothing, you will need to get on your face and ask God to forgive the transgressions of your father, mother, grandparents; because somewhere in the past someone did something and it has trickled down to you.

Again, since the beginning of the Word, we have been told that God punishes the children to the third and fourth generations (Exodus 20:5+). So clean up the mess in your life and start living one of true repentance.

Romans 1:18

The wrath of God is being revealed against all the godlessness and wickedness of men who suppress the truth by their wickedness...! (NIV)

CHAPTER FOUR

Revelation

Galatians 5:16-20

So, I say, live by the Spirit, and you will not gratify the desires of the sinful nature. For the sinful nature desires what is contrary to the Spirit, and the Spirit what is contrary to the sinful nature. They are in conflict with each other, so that you do not do what you want. But if you are led by the Spirit you are not under law.

The acts of the sinful nature are obvious: sexual immorality, impurity and debauchery; idolatry and witchcraft; hatred, discord, jealousy, fits of rage, selfish ambition, dissentions, factions and envy; drunkenness, orgies, and the like.

I warn you, as I did before, that those that live like this will not inherit the kingdom of God. (NIV)

Do you constantly seek out money, position, that person you want to have an affair with? Are you a control freak or a complainer-bringing down everyone around you? Showing your lack of faith and joy in the Lord?

Again, so many people want to discount the Old Testament and focus on the New because they think that Jesus's life and death changed the demand for purity, but we are to study the Israelites' past to see what is required of us and to see what God did to His number one, chosen people.

The Old Testament is there to teach us and warn us about choosing to live a life against God, which is what quite a few Christians do. Many, in fact, think they are standing firm when actually, they follow the Devil's leadings at his slightest urging.

Paul wanted us to know, in Galatians 1, that the gospel preached isn't something he made up. That it wasn't taken from any man, but that he received it by revelation from Jesus Christ.

We need to get a revelation of how the Holy Spirit is really telling us to live. Don't settle for listening to what some man on a pulpit tells us, because it may not be the whole truth, and certainly don't listen to what our flesh wants to tell us because the nature of man is evil.

We need to develop our consciences to work in accordance with our Holy Spirit so we can get it right.

I hear so many people who have never read the Bible tell me that they are able to do any horrible thing against the blood of Jesus and the will of God, and still be considered good, God-fearing Christians. How can a person continuously doing bad things be considered good? That might be a misconception. Is it worth the risk?

So, with scriptures from the book of Revelation, which we agree is the last word of prophesy, let's see what the disciple John has to say.

John revealed in his letters to the churches (of which we are) that it is a man who walks in the ways the Lord commands who will go to Heaven. Who are true Christians and not Pharisees.

Revelation 2:2

I know your works, your labor and patience, and how you cannot bear evil men, and you have tried those who say they are apostles but are not and have found them liars. (KJV)

I'm all for forgiveness. We should forgive all men all things, but just because you want to forgive the cheating pastor, youth minister, priest, that does not mean that you leave this abomination in possession of the holy Word of God and in leadership of what is supposed to be your holy church.

The Bible says that they have defiled themselves and are to no longer touch the sacraments or teach God's holy Words. You do not leave someone who has failed the test in that important position.

Forgive them all you want, but do not let them continue in the position they have now contaminated. See Ezekiel 44:10,13; 1 Timothy 3:1-10; Titus 1:7-11; Acts 20:26-31; Romans 2:19-24; 1 Corinthians 4:1.

2 Corinthians 11:13-15

...For such men are false prophets, deceitful workmen, masquerading as apostles of Christ. And no wonder, for Satan himself masquerades as an angel of light. It is not surprising, then, if his servants masquerade as servants of righteousness. Their end will be what their actions deserve. (NIV)

Be very careful who you choose to follow. If their actions, their fruit, does not show the required level of righteousness, then do not let them remain in that holy position of church leader.

I have heard people excuse the adulterous church leader or elder by saying that he's only a man. Well then fire him and let him go be just a man. If he wants to be like every other heathen out there, he doesn't belong at the pulpit. Do not be afraid to expect more of your religious leaders.

And be careful not to adopt the ways of an evil man. You must warn him and get away from him so as not to be tempted yourselves (Galatians 6:1). If you see people who bear no fruit, do no good works, have no love, you can probably safely say that it is not wise to adapt their ways, no matter how spiritual or religious they profess themselves to be.

People cannot earn acceptance into God's family, but they certainly have to work at being allowed to stay.

Revelation 2:7

He that has an ear, let him hear what the Spirit says to the churches. To him who overcomes, will I give the right to eat from the tree of life, which is in midst of the paradise of God. (KJV)

Revelation 2:10

...Be faithful, even to your death, and I will give you the crown of life. (KJV)

Revelation 2:16-17

Repent! Or else I will come to you quickly and fight against you with the sword of my mouth. He who has an ear let him hear what the Spirit says to the churches. To him that overcomes, I will give some of the hidden manna to eat... (KJV)

Revelation 3:1-2

...I know your deeds; you have a reputation of being alive but you are dead. Wake up! Strengthen what remains and is about to die, for I have not found your deeds complete in the sight of my God. (NIV)

Revelation 3:10

Since you have kept my command to endure patiently, I will also keep you from the hour of trial that is going to come upon the whole world to test those who live on the earth. (NIV)

Revelation 3:21-22

To him who overcomes, I will grant to sit with me on my throne, even as I overcame and sat down with my Father in His throne. He who has an ear, let him hear what the Spirit says to the churches. (KJV)

If Jesus went to the extent of death to overcome self-want, surely we can learn to control our feelings, then our actions, and do right.

John tells that it was ordered not to harm the land, the sea, or the trees until a seal is put on the foreheads of the servants of our God.

Look at your life and see who you truly serve. Sin is the work of the Devil and if you are giving in to his demands, his temptations, then you are not a servant of the Lord.

As Jesus said, you cannot serve two masters (Luke 16:13). One or the other has to lose. Pray that Jesus is the one you let win in every situation.

Do you make excuses for the Devil's ways as he rules your life? For the fits, the bad feelings, the grudges, the sin? You should make Jesus your ruler and turn all of these feelings over to God immediately so that you don't risk them growing into pain for you or for another.

Saying, "No one's perfect, we're only human," is giving Satan and your sinful nature the chance to manipulate and rule you. You must instead tell yourself, "I will be perfect, as my Lord Jesus, whom I follow, is perfect," and in doing so, give yourself the strength to overcome. For he who does not overcome has no place at the banquet the Father has prepared for us.

Revelation 14:3-5

And they sang a new song before the throne...No one could learn the song accept the 144,000 who had been redeemed from the earth. These are those who did not defile themselves with women (**or men**) for they kept themselves pure...No lie was found in their mouths, they are blameless. (NIV)

Revelation 14:9-11

And the third angel said in a loud voice, "If any man worships the beast and his image and receives his mark in their forehead or in his hand, they shall drink the wine of God's wrath, which is poured into the cup of His indignation. And he shall be tormented with fire and brimstone in the presence of the holy angels and of the Lamb. And the smoke of their torment goes up for ever and ever; and they have no rest, day or night, those who worship the beast and his image, and whoever receives the mark of his name." (KJV)

Our actions are a form of worship. Whom do yours honor? Do you run around consciously or unconsciously doing the work of Satan? All sin is the desire of the Devil, and nothing pleases Satan more then to see God's people serving his evil desires. Stop giving him the satisfaction and right yourself.

People who don't meaningfully serve Satan are still going to receive his mark because they followed him so many times throughout their 'Christian' lives. The adulterous pastor; the perverted priest; the back-stabbing elder; the youth minister who lusts after the teens he has chosen to lead; the gossipy secretary; the selfish, compassionless, and unkind congregation.

Those who don't act in the love and righteousness of God might be in for a terrible shock on judgment day, when all of their horrible secrets and the motives of their hearts are revealed for all to see.

And John's description of Hades isn't a pretty picture either.

I always describe it like this, think of the worst experience you have ever had. One that cut your heart in two. Most people can think of at least one, other people can do some pretty heartless and cruel things in our lives. Now imagine that horrible pain never going away, no relief from that suffering, never healing, only the constant torment of the event day in and day out. There would be some weeping and gnashing of teeth if you never healed from your wounds or your heartache, not to mention the threat of burning continuously.

Revelation 14:12-13

Here is the patience of the saints, those who obey God's commandments and the faith of Jesus. And I heard a voice from heaven say, "Write, blessed are the dead which die in the Lord from this day on." "Yes, says the Spirit, "they may rest from their labors, for their works do follow them." (KJV)

In Revelation 19, it says we are to rejoice and be glad, and also give God praise because the wedding of the Lamb has come, and that the bride has made herself ready.

As the Bible says, God's chosen, the church, is the bride. Do you remember the often-quoted parable of the ten virgins in Matthew 25? They missed the wedding because they weren't prepared. And the wedding banquet, where the one that was brought in in place of those invited, but was not dressed properly, and so was thrown back out.

Consider this, which do you think is worse: the unmarried man who meets a woman and has an affair with her or the married man who meets a woman and has an affair with her? It is in this same way that the believer who sins is far worse than the unbeliever who does.

The unbeliever is ignorant, but the child of God is chosen to be above the dregs of this world of sin. They are cheating on the glorious Lord who chose them as his bride and have shown their unfaithfulness. And therefore, they chance a divorce from him because they are not trustworthy. They may just be condemning themselves to eternal damnation.

Revelation 16:15

"Behold, I come like a thief! Blessed is he who stays awake and keeps his clothes with him, so that he may not go naked and be shamefully exposed." (NIV)

Revelation 20:7-8

...Satan will be set free from his prison and shall go out to deceive the nations... (NIV)

Everyone who has sold you that lie of abusing God's forgiveness and grace has tricked you into giving yourself freedom to sin. It is not the truth. It is a lie that Satan himself slipped into the church with misinterpretations of scripture to this poor me, feel good society so that his sin, his ways will continue to reign.

Do not allow yourselves to be deceived any longer. Anyone with sin in their heart is unclean. You must walk as the Father commands. You must learn to control every emotion and action in a manner that shows respect and appreciation to God for choosing you from among the millions.

Remember:

Romans 12:1

I beg you brothers, by the mercies of God, that you present your bodies as a living sacrifice, holy and acceptable to God- this is your reasonable act of worship. (KJV)

Revelation 20:12-13

And I saw the dead...stand before God...The dead were judged out of those things that were written in the books, according to their works. And the sea gave up the dead which were in it, and death and Hell delivered up the dead which were in them, and they were judged according to their works. (KJV)

So when your book is opened and God says, "I see here that I gave you My Spirit, I covered you with the blood of My Son, yet you chose to give in to your fleshy desires and so trample him under foot, crucify him again and again, knowing what you would receive for that..." what fate is coming to you? That which you were promised.

God never promised us Heaven in exchange for sin. He has said since the beginning of time that sin brings death. Sin brings curses. At no point did He ever promise us eternal life in exchange for sin. Jesus did not die for us to live a life of sin and get away with it.

This idea that God will forgive someone who goes to church and simply says, "Jesus is Lord," but does not show that they believe in the life that he or she lives is helping to cause the fall once again.

And so, just like back in the beginning, even God's holy people allow themselves to be defiled with sin and help spread the lie that sin is acceptable to God.

Since you are blessed with the Spirit of God, when sin tempts you, try to say, "No way! I love God and I will not kill Jesus again. Jesus is my strength against Satan's schemes. It is out of love for God and Jesus-and whoever that sin is going to hurt, whether it be you or someone else-that I will not be tempted to do what I know I'm not supposed to do."

Revelation 21:7-8

He who overcomes will inherit all this, and I will be his God and he will be my son. But the cowardly, the unbelieving, the vile, the murderers, the sexually immoral, those who practice the magic arts, the idolaters and all liars- their place will be in the fiery lake of burning sulfur. This is the second death. (NIV)

Revelation 21:27

Nothing impure will ever enter it (the new Jerusalem), nor will anyone who does what is shameful or deceitful, but only those whose names are written in the Lamb's book of life. (NIV)

Revelation 22:12-15

"Behold, I come quickly! And my reward is with me, to give to every man according to his works...Blessed are those that do His commandments, that they may have the right to the tree of life and may go through the gates into the city. Outside are the dogs, sorcerers, fornicators and adulterers, murderers, idolaters, and whoever loves and makes up lies. (KJV)

CHAPTER FIVE

Love

So many sermons are about God loving us, but again, it is important to look at the other side of the coin. What about our love for God? This narcissistic society rarely thinks of what is going out from us. The focus is usually on what's coming our way. That has led us to the current state of the me generation. The Bible says that you reap what you sow. You have to sow first your time, your heart, your thoughts, your compassion, and your understanding. Get out of the selfish walk that comes naturally to our human nature and start giving of yourself.

If you have been called, and long to seek God, and call yourself a Christian, the first step is serving others, not waiting on what you think you are going to get from God. The one thing Jesus told us to do is to love our neighbor. That is what he said time and time again is the greatest commandment.

So if you have asked Jesus to come into your life, then your heart toward others must change. If I want to do a certain thing, but in the end it will hurt another for me to have my way, I have to let go of that desire so that I don't wander into idolatry.

Just look at 1 Corinthians 13. If we speak in tongues but don't act with love, it's just useless noise. If we can prophesy and have abounding faith but no love, we are nothing. Even if we give our money to the poor but do not have love, we gain nothing. You have to really care for the people around you. Your treatment of people can't just be an act.

We also must go beyond simply loving our family and good friends.

In Matthew 5, Jesus says that to be children of God we have to love our enemies and pray for those who persecute us. The Bible tells us that anyone is able to love those close to them, but the reward is in loving everyone.

The hardest verses are probably Luke 6:27-31. We are told to love our enemies, do good to haters, bless when cursed, and pray for all. Also, to give give give, but the last line of that scripture gives us a hint how to do so and is so beneficial to our Christian walk. Do to others as you want it done to you. We need to take a breath and think, okay I was wronged, but if the shoe was on the other foot, how would I want that coming back to me if I messed up?

Why would God tell us to love one another? As in the Scripture "love covers over a multitude of sins," the act of extending love to others will, many times, keep us from wrongdoing. It's important to think about the Word and what it's trying to tell us. Try to focus on what the Bible says, not how we feel about different situations we are faced with.

We have to be careful what we let our minds dwell on and the roads we let our thoughts travel down. This situation happened at work, it's upsetting, but rather than roll it over again and again in your brain, jump into the Word and read about how to handle that issue. Someone wronged you, ouch! But don't stew. Pray for them and ask God to help you get over that offense. Sin starts in your mind, but so does love. Which will you let win in your soul? As those thoughts come into our minds, immediately bombard them with good things that are in our lives. Fight depression with joy and the promises in the Bible. The Devil is persistent, so the notion will keep coming back. Be more stubborn and combat bad images and ideals with positive, joyful, and righteous thinking. Learn to change the channel in your mind quickly so that evil doesn't take root.

One thing each of us needs to understand is that the world does not revolve around us. All of Romans 13 tells us that we have fulfilled the law if we live our lives loving others, because we've put others above ourselves. That is Jesus's whole message. Love your neighbor.

If attacked, just slow down in taking offense. Rather, consider what that person may be going through in their life. What could be happening to them that made them lash out? Although there is no excuse for treating people poorly, we need to pause a moment and not only think about how we have been made to feel. Stop and find peace in the fact that our day is great and things are going our way, then use that to show understanding to our neighbor. That is the first step in learning to walk in love. Aren't you happy when God forgives you? Others deserve that from us. And what are we told? If we do not forgive, our father won't forgive us our trespasses.

That is why we have to be careful about judging others from the negative side of how they are acting. Judging them by how they've made us feel rather than considering their possible problems.

How does it make you feel when you mess up and do something stupid, say something stupid, and the guy on the receiving end is gracious, kind, and forgiving when they respond with understanding and react with love, instead of coming back at you? The Bible says a kind word turns away wrath. We also should practice that. Respond with love even when attacked. Not only will it defuse the attacker, but we won't have sinned against the command God and Jesus gave us to walk in love. Remember blessings come when blessings are going out from us.

Do you bother listening to what God is trying to tell you through your Spirit or have you hardened your heart so much because of the things that have happened to you in your life that you exist in pity party mode and you are unable to hear His voice any longer? If every time something happens to you you go on the attack and it's more important to win the argument and get your point across, then something is wrong in you and you may not truly have the Holy Spirit. Just as if you continue in your life of sin you are only a surface Christian. You may not have God's Spirit because you would start thinking differently. You would no longer desire to do the things that benefit Satan rather than

God or Jesus. That is why Romans 12:9 tells us that love must be sincere and that we should hate what is evil and hold to what is good. Live in love to each other and put others above our own wants.

God loved us so much that He sacrificed His son. Won't we even love God enough to sacrifice a desire, a bad habit, a handful of ideals that are no good for us anyway? If you drink too much and die from your alcoholism, you haven't acted in love toward the people who love you and want you in their life. You haven't loved God and the gift He gave you of life. Even just the fact you woke up today and got out of bed should be acknowledged and focused on, rather than all the griefs and hardships of life.

We need to thank God for the little things all day because there are many in the world who did not receive that simple blessing that we are taking for granted. We need to stop feeling sorry for ourselves because everything in our lives isn't perfect. There are others with far less than we have.

Do you notice all the little signs of love that God is sending you throughout the day? It's easy to ignore, but pay attention. Did you bother looking at the radiant blue of the sky or the flowers that happened to blow up on to your doorstep? Did you notice the beneficial coincidences that came just when you needed them and call them what they are? Little gifts from God. Did you notice the ping of joy in your heart and let that happiness grow to envelope your day? That's God saying hello. It's too easy to focus on the negative but it's so important to cling to the little things that are going our way and give thanks for them, so that they can multiply.

Remember, what we feed grows. Don't feed the sin, don't feed the bad that we all face. Hold to the good and water it so that there is more and more of it coming our way. Life gets better the more joy and good we have in our lives, and happiness gives us strength. We need it to overcome the drudgery and start living better lives.

Can't we sacrifice our human nature so that we can become true Christians with a Spirit receptive to the truths of the Bible?

It's not even about going to heaven or facing damnation. It's a question of why you would want to be a human being who's a git, a wretch, and of no benefit to society. Are you helping the world become a better place and live in love, or are you just another person helping to bring destruction to man's existence by spewing hatred and ignorance, keeping the fight alive, helping the Devil take over?

These days the world is so full of hostility and common sense has all but disappeared from the masses. God is real, but even for those who do not want to believe in Him, they can look at the Bible as simply a moral code. It's a book full of common sense that leads us to live a better life and a how to to treat others the right way.

Just look at all the children killing other children. Look at the bullying. That's because God was taken out of our schools. It's because so many of our teachers now are on the other side of Christianity and they are the people our children spend the greatest portion of their day with. And parents are too busy working multiple jobs to make ends meet, so that they are always exhausted, stressed out, and not raising their children anymore-television is. And it's a medium mostly controlled and used by evil people bent on corrupting us and the next generation.

T.V., violent video games, and violent music are the babysitters of this generation. If the only thing you feed your children is sugar and fast food, and the only thing you're feeding their spirits is sex, violence and forms of anything-is-acceptable-if-you-want-it ideals, the end result is what we see in our schools these days. Feed your children healthy food, feed them God, and His teachings, a great moral code, and the love Jesus commanded us to give, and we'll see a difference in our future.

Our young adults are paying for the distance government has put between us and God with a bad economy, endless violence in our streets and schools, more drug abuse and mental health issues, and fewer and fewer blessings. Being raised without God's moral code has created a great divide between God's prosperity and goodness and the current state of life we are living.

Get a clue and get back with God, but follow the word and do not make the mistake of deciding which sins are okay to commit and which are not. None of them are okay and all sin will cause grief and stress in our lives.

And then, what if He is real and you've made the mistake of turning your back on Him your whole life? Discounting yourself from all the blessings that serving God provides and all the joy and happiness that He is able to fill your life with? People today are so crazy, rude, and self-centered and it's because we as a society are getting further and further from God, driving Jesus out of our lives. Not only not being raised with his teachings, but sometimes simply by being too busy to love him and enjoy our lives.

Even those who have been called turn their backs on him by going their own way. But remember Jesus died on a cross like a common criminal even though he was innocent, so that we could come into the family of God, a family that promotes kindness and love, prosperity and righteousness. Don't make his sacrifice a waste. Understand that he loved people so much that he literally died for us.

What then will you do with the knowledge of that sacrifice? Keep sinning? Keep treating people horribly? Continue to be thankless for all you do have? That's a slap in his face and why would he then cherish or love you? And more so, why would you want to oppose the most important ideal Jesus gave us? Love.

In John 15:12, just as we are told we must resist sin to the point of shedding our own blood, we are also told that we are to love to the point of laying down our lives for our neighbors and friends. But if you gossip, cheat, curse, sin, steal, kill, you are going against every command Jesus gave us and what benefit do you think that will get you? None.

Proverbs says many claim to have love but who can find a faithful person? The righteous lead blameless lives. Blessed are their children. With a human nature, sometimes accidents do happen. If one is running through the house and rams their toe on the corner of the couch leg and shouts out expletives, that probably falls into the blameless category. But if one goes on a tirade against another and cusses them out, they are exerting no self-control and fall into purposeful sins. It's easy to voice that comeback, but sometimes we need to just be quiet. Get in the practice when given the opportunity to say something, don't, because that gives the other person an opportunity to come back at you. Thus, the train keeps going around the mountain and the fight continues. Wouldn't it be better to just remain silent and forgive, so as not to play volleyball with hurtful comments that could escalate into a greater confrontation?

At some point we must control ourselves. The Bible says that love casts out fear. You don't have to fear because you live in love, but if you are treating people badly you're not living in love, and if you are sinning, you're not showing love for Jesus.

Deuteronomy 7:9-11

Know therefore that the Lord your God is God; He is the faithful God, keeping his covenant of love to a thousand generations of those who love him and keep His commands. But those who hate Him He will repay to their face by destruction; He will not be slow to repay to their face those who hate Him. Therefore, take care to follow the commands and decrees and laws I give you today. (NIV)

Look at your life and gauge how things are going. There are a multitude of blessings waiting in the service of God, but are you seeking Him if you are not loving people and learning not to sin? Will you then receive the good things promised in the Word?

Get over that greedy spirit that thinks you're owed anything. You get what you give, not only in blessings and finances, but also in curses. Look back at Leviticus 26 and see how God will come against you if you are purposefully going at Him. Why would you want to live that way? Why wouldn't you want to live on the joyous side of Jesus? Where even if you're not getting blessed, you at least have peace about what is coming against you.

Fighting sin and our human nature is such a battle. It is so hard, but at some point, we are expected to grow up. It is so easy to believe that we can stay baby Christians our whole lives, but is that true? If we are required to walk in love, as was Jesus greatest command but never do, are we really following Jesus? 1 Corinthians 13 tells us that when we are children, we can talk and think like children, but when we become adults, we put childish ways behind us. It also says that our past becomes like an image in a mirror, but now we see things face to face. Life becomes real. Then we knew in part; now we must know fully. The three things that remain after we shed the selfishness of our childhood are faith, hope, and the most important thing, love.

Proverbs advises us that we should never let love or faith leave us, but should write them in our hearts. Then we will have favor in the sight of God and man.

Somehow, we have to dial down the crazy in this society. Satan is after us, for nothing more than to cause us grief and sit back and laugh as we writhe in agony from the repercussions of making bad decisions. If he gets you to make a mistake, then he gets the joy of watching you ache in pain for it. He's like the naughty little kid causing his father grief. Why would you want to follow him and why do you allow yourself to be tricked into going against the common sense that we are blessed with with the Holy Spirit by an acceptance of sin? This poor me society needs to grow up and start living lives that show love and kindness to all around us. If everyone treated people with compassion and truly cared for others, the world would be a much better place.

You can't do evil things against the word of God and think you're in the right. Right is right and wrong is wrong. Don't be led astray by some cable news show or popular public figure that is actually leading you into ignorance and into sinning against people trying to do the right thing and help. Seek God and you will be blessed with wisdom to see through people's, and the Devil's, tricks.

Every human being should be doing what is proper and kind to the people around them. They should accept the consequences for not doing right. You don't have to pay for what you don't do wrong; there is no repercussion for doing the right thing all the time. Everyone should be helping the poor and less fortunate so crime isn't a necessity for so many. Parents should instill values and class into their children and teach them to always do the right thing. They are the next leaders of our world and if they are taught selfishness, wildness, and no common sense, never learning to see the right in situations and think logically for themselves, where will we be then? Exactly where we are now and headed for worse.

Goodness is goodness, sin is sin, evil is evil no matter how sorry you feel for yourself to then allow yourself to do wrong or treat someone badly. And God hates it all.

You will be judged on every word you say (Matthew 12:36) and every person you help to live a life of sin. Know that you will be held accountable for their blood (Genesis 9:5 and Ezekiel 33). Make sure that you aren't one of the unwitting minions of Satan who have helped spread the lie of an everlasting acceptance of sin and allowance of walking an evil and hateful walk.

So, when you talk to others or see someone giving themselves an excuse to go against God, I hope you can save them with the truth. Study the Word of God. Live a life that will be pleasing to God and to others. Exalt and uplift yourself and others, and try to be righteous, not just make each other feel good about nothing. We need to offer each other God's requirements and truth and expect more. More Spirit, more righteousness, more strength, more zeal, and therefore, more peace and joy in the Lord.

God believes in you. Step out in the Name and in the righteousness of the Lord! Now go read the Bible, read books by upright, prosperous, and decent people serving God and may God bless us all!

Ephesians 6:10-11, 13-17

Finally, be strong in the Lord and in His mighty power. Put on the full armor of God so that you can take your stand against the devil's schemes...put on the full armor of God, so that when the day of evil comes, you may be able to stand your ground, and after you have done everything, to stand. Stand firm then, with the belt of truth buckled around your waist, with the breastplate of righteousness in place, and with your feet fitted with the readiness that comes from the gospel of peace. In addition to all this, take up the shield of faith, with which you can extinguish all the flaming arrows of the evil one. Take the helmet of salvation and the sword of the Spirit, which is the word of God.

(NIV)

Printed in the United States
By Bookmasters